Human Rights Interventions

Series Editors
Chiseche Mibenge
Stanford University
Stanford, CA, USA

Irene Hadiprayitno
Leiden University
Leiden, Zuid-Holland, The Netherlands

The traditional human rights frame creates a paradigm by which the duty bearer's (state) and rights holder's (civil society organizations) interests collide over the limits of enjoyment and enforcement. The series departs from the paradigm by centering peripheral yet powerful actors that agitate for intervention and influence in the (re)shaping of rights discourse in the midst of grave insecurities. The series privileges a call and response between theoretical inquiry and empirical investigation as contributors critically assess human rights interventions mediated by spatial, temporal, geopolitical and other dimensions. An interdisciplinary dialogue is key as the editors encourage multiple approaches such as law and society, political economy, historiography, legal ethnography, feminist security studies, and multi-media.

More information about this series at
http://www.palgrave.com/gp/series/15595

Joel R. Pruce

The Mass Appeal of Human Rights

palgrave
macmillan

Joel R. Pruce
Department of Political Science
University of Dayton
Dayton, OH, USA

Human Rights Interventions
ISBN 978-3-030-06357-3 ISBN 978-3-319-92075-7 (eBook)
https://doi.org/10.1007/978-3-319-92075-7

Cover design: Laura de Grasse

Printed on acid-free paper

This Palgrave Macmillan imprint is published by the registered company Springer International Publishing AG part of Springer Nature
The registered company address is: Gewerbestrasse 11, 6330 Cham, Switzerland

To Heather Anne, forevermore.

Preface

When you work on a project for long enough, the present becomes the past and the past becomes the distant past. But the future remains the future and only once we cross over into the future do we approach a position from which we can proffer a sober assessment; just as Hegel and his owl suggest. This project always felt to me that it was of the present, a critical examination of a phenomenon that was all around us, in the headlines and in our news feeds. Now that I've completed it, I am increasingly curious whether what I've prepared here is a time capsule of a period in the rearview rather than a snapshot out my window.[1]

I grew up in human rights attending local chapter meetings of Amnesty International. I formed a chapter in my New Jersey high school and my college roommate and I ran our campus chapter. After college, I moved to the West Coast and staked out an active chapter there, like someone in recovery looking for a meeting. In graduate school, my study of human rights deepened as did my skepticism of the enterprise. The Save Darfur movement of 2004–2007 provoked me initially, transforming my skepticism into suspicion. I finished the first iteration of this book in 2012, when "Make Joseph Kony Famous" swept us off our feet—a campaign that appeared as proof-of-concept for the argument I was developing. Now, looking backward and forward, I wonder if anything

[1] I'm indebted to an anonymous reviewer for Palgrave who brought this question to my attention and challenged me to consider the passage of time.

approximating the groundswell of energy behind Save Darfur or Kony 2012 will ever manifest again. Has human rights lost its mass appeal?

The work for this book began the week of President Obama's inauguration, only to wrap in the second year of the Trump administration; a period pregnant with hope bookended by a wave of fear. It was to be an era of recovery following the belligerent interventions of the Bush administration, however sympathetic even he was to certain human rights causes, including Darfur. Obama promised to right the ship of state and re-orient American power behind liberal internationalist values. But American power and will had grown tepid by this point, more so than human rights advocates may have preferred. In crucial ways, it took the human rights community over ten years to realize that the 1990s had ended. In that time, the USA had squandered whatever moral currency it may have had and encountered a soured world turning increasingly to new sources of support and searching for alternative frameworks. Panned as weak and dithering, Obama's paralysis provided fertile ground for the rise of Trump's bellicose cries—a reaction to the failures of internationalism to extend and protect US interests. Not only were the 1990s over, but finally the age of Jimmy Carter, the first post-cold war president, was also slammed shut. The intervening period witnessed its share of mass atrocities, but no mass movements. Syria, Myanmar, Central African Republic, Yemen, and Mexico are only the most egregious horror shows and despite condemnation, reporting, and efforts to mobilize, none took hold of the hearts of advocates.

This book, in many ways, is about the USA because the USA, its culture, its society, and its politics, are the center of the global human rights universe; which is a descriptive statement, not a normative one. As others have argued, the prospects for transnational human rights advocacy rose and fell with the US hegemon. Yet human rights have not, as still others have argued, receded, or expired, but have taken new form and have come to occupy new spaces. Regional networks gain strength. National human rights institutions continue to spring up around the world, including in post-conflict and transitional societies. Local movements fly the flag in their confrontation with the increasingly hostile forces of provincialism and chauvinism. Human rights continues to be recontextualized and re-articulated in the lives and struggles of marginalized groups. This is equally true in the USA.

For instance, the collective demand that Black lives should matter to police officers, before the criminal justice system, and in the eyes of society at large is a declaration that African Americans be counted as equals in the human family. Yes, "mattering" instructs that the subject be treated with the respect due to any being with inherent dignity and worth. No, all US movements for racial justice do not uniformly adopt the human rights banner. But delegations representing critical communities, including from Ferguson and Chicago, have pursued accountability through global human rights mechanisms, and these efforts signal the persistent appeal of making internationalized rights-based claims. The power of these initiatives may be even more acute, essential, and forthcoming in an age of US decline and retrenchment.

As the Trump agenda rolled out, ugly and clumsy, impacted constituencies came together, often working across identity groups to forge new intersectional coalitions. Yes, there are fault lines and disagreements. No, there is not consensus that human rights best captures the claim for everyone in every instance. But the expression that "(fill-in-the-blank) Rights are Human Rights" is a ubiquitous phrase on the placards of protestors as the most basic request for recognition and I think that means something. The energy, momentum, and sheer quantity of grassroots political activity suggest that the demographics that may have previously been moved by a transnational advocacy campaign for the human rights of distant strangers are now focused on their local context and even on threats to their own rights. The 2017 Women's March is the clearest evidence of this possibility and of the potential for a furious population to reclaim sovereignty over its politics, even in an age of polarization and cynicism.

Human rights may be experiencing the same contraction as other globalizing forces have exhibited but contraction for human rights does not mean disappearance or death. Rather, human rights may become reinterpreted and relocated in ways that can help secure their future. Transnationalism could return at any time because all the tools and platforms endure. The truly threatening proposition holds that if human rights are reinvigorated by their resurgence at the local and national levels, then new transnational advocacy networks may emerge with deeper roots and more forceful resolve. Until that future materializes, we can look back on the mass appeal of human rights as a manufactured symptom of a moment when ordinary people genuinely believed they could change the world.

Dayton, OH, USA
April 2018

Joel R. Pruce

Acknowledgements

This book is the product of years of conversations, debates, questions, elevator pitches, and self-doubt. While all the empirical mistakes and errors in judgment are my own, I have benefited tremendously from relationships with many people. Stephen Eric Bronner is my earliest intellectual inspiration and mentor. Micheline Ishay challenged me to think critically and dialectically. Jack Donnelly guided me with his precise style. Roger Haydon pushed me to write more assertively and dedicated significant effort to improving this project. I am also indebted to colleagues and friends who provided input and support along the way: George Andreopolous, Zehra F. Kabasakal Arat, Tristan Anne Borer, Alexandra C. Budabin, Natalie F. Hudson, Rachael Liberman, Jonathan Moyer, Grant Neeley, Marilyn Pruce, James Ron, Marc Ross, and Daniel J. Whelan.

This book is dedicated to Heather Atkinson who epitomizes why writers—particularly academic writers—thank their partners. This book is unimaginable without her. Heather has been my pep-talker, cheerleader, and champion from the beginning: defending my dissertation, adopting our dog, taking my first job, getting married, moving across the country for a second job, buying our first home, having our two children, Wyatt and Daisy, and now publishing this book. Everything is due to her and I am grateful, forevermore.

Contents

CHAPTER 1

Introduction: "You, Elie Wiesel, and Paris Hilton"

On December 10, 2009, I received an email with a provocative subject line—"You, Elie Wiesel, and Paris Hilton." The message was distributed to the listserv of the Genocide Intervention Network and delivered over the signature of Executive Director Sam Bell. An unlikely threesome, the characters referenced in the email's subject were all familiar: I, at the time an angst-ridden graduate student; Elie Wiesel, Auschwitz witness, Nobel Laureate in Literature, and anti-genocide crusader; and Paris Hilton, billionaire heiress, reality television star, and fashion icon who rose to cultural prominence for her role in a leaked sex-tape. The organization sought new supporters for a fledgling movement coalescing around the prevention of mass atrocities and genocide, to which Mr. Wiesel and Ms. Hilton recently pledged their names. The email also advertised ongoing canvassing efforts and upcoming events designed to build an educated constituent base. That evening, on the sixty-first anniversary of the adoption of the Universal Declaration of Human Rights, the US Holocaust Memorial Museum hosted a Webcast interview with Susan Rice, Permanent Representative to the United Nations, and "you" were invited to participate.

Curious as it may seem, strategic communication carries meaning. Embedded messaging profits from and reproduces prevailing resonance within the audience. Elie Wiesel's presence symbolizes the gravity of the crisis. His experience as a survivor of Nazi brutality and poignant translator of horror lends credibility. Paris Hilton stands in as a recognizable face bringing style and cachet to the campaign, while injecting levity and

J. R. Pruce, *The Mass Appeal of Human Rights*, Human Rights Interventions, https://doi.org/10.1007/978-3-319-92075-7_1

seduction. Her association signals that the issue is cool and sexy, permitting the young and uninitiated a portal to the cause. Perhaps most importantly, though, "you" are the primary subject of the communication. "You" stand equally besides Elie Wiesel and Paris Hilton in your shared desire to propel genocide prevention to the top of the foreign policy agenda. "You" represent not only individual agency, but also the multitude of "yous" who, together, will bring an end to the crime of crimes. "You, Elie Wiesel, and Paris Hilton" is an unironic vision statement of a listless movement striving to be all things to all people. A context in which this unholy trinity can be seamlessly woven together—in which a Holocaust survivor and sex-tape debutante can occupy the same space without raising alarms—prompts critical questions about the manifestation of human rights at the intersection of global affairs and consumer society.

The bizarre juxtaposition of solemnity and stardom, the macabre and the erotic, emerges as the culmination of a legacy of human rights advocacy that fuses political demands with popular trends. Every crisis generates a celebrity solicitation, benefit telethon, or ad campaign requesting urgent donations. As routine as this relationship has become to a twenty-first-century observer, many assumptions at the foundation of this strategic approach to mass mobilization remain unquestioned. For instance, what makes Paris Hilton an acceptable ambassador for genocide prevention? What qualifications does she possess? What resources does she offer? How does her sordid reputation affect the public assertions of the Genocide Intervention Network?

It suffices to say that with no background in foreign policy, or expertise in the areas of conflict, mass violence, or transnational politics, she is not an obvious candidate. And more so, the vapid persona she cultivates sits in stark contrast to the severity of the problem she seeks to address. Hilton's presence alongside a stoic and revered figure like Wiesel could reasonably damage the integrity of the campaign if audiences interpret her endorsement as a cheap attempt by the organization to entice and arouse. Situating Paris Hilton as an inspirational human rights hero presumes that the intended targets will either overlook her salacious qualities or, instead, come for the sex appeal and stay for the human suffering.

This book exposes the awkward, uneasy, and problematic convergence of consumer culture and human rights. Substantively and at their core, human rights campaigns assert controversial arguments about the importance of human dignity in the face of the arbitrary exercise of power.

Protest movements for social change challenge the dominant order, advancing new normative priorities. Emancipatory struggles insist on the transformation of structures and institutions, and aspire to a future of equality and autonomy. The history of human rights is indeed a history of confrontation between forces seeking to preserve the status quo and those acting in defense of the marginalized. Revolutionaries across the ages rallied around rights claims as proclamations of their need for respect and recognition, and following the Second World War, these articulations served as the hopeful cornerstones for peace and decency. To do the work of human rights is to be somehow linked to inherently political and subversive. Human rights are not conciliatory or ambivalent assertions. Human rights norms propose an ideal world that looks dramatically different from ours and advocates call for this world to be born.

Despite this history of resistance and contestation, the Paris Hilton model is not novel or without precedent, even if it is a lascivious example. Human rights groups have commonly deployed creative strategies for expanding their reach and raising their profile. Dating back to the abolition of the slave trade and through the Free Congo Movement at the turn of the twentieth century, political pleas were conveyed by well-known figures, captured in graphic visual images, and framed using catchy slogans. Here, we can consider the participation of Sir Arthur Conan Doyle and Mark Twain, photographs of the severed limbs of Congolese at the hands of Belgian *Force Publique*, and the circulation of "Am I Not a Man and a Brother?" stamps. Twenty-first-century human rights marketing owes a debt to nineteenth-century campaigners and tracing this lineage requires historicity while appreciating its contemporary shift. Today, elements of mass media and popular culture are integral to human rights advocacy and serve as central features of outreach, fund-raising, and movement-building efforts. The integration of mass culture into human rights practice calls into question the contentious nature of human rights claims and creates a new tradition, a new trajectory.

Human rights advocacy is no longer reserved merely for dissidents or diplomats. What was an agitated rallying cry for fairness and justice is now also a key component of the mainstream moral imagination. Particularly as embodied in the work of major transnational nongovernmental organizations (NGOs), human rights have become integrated as products of privileged lifestyles, accommodating rather than challenging structures of inequality. To engage in human rights advocacy today is to participate in a practice once proprietary to iconoclasts and lawyers but now subsumed within daily rituals of consumers and television audiences. The practice has in fact been incorporated into habits of average individuals in a way that makes the performance commonplace and undisruptive to everyday life. One need not invest profound commitments of time, energy, or anguish in order to take part (or feel as though one is taking part) in the protection of someone else's human dignity.

Human rights advocacy consists in simple acts, not heroic feats. No barricades or sit-ins. No threats of bodily harm or civil disobedience. Direct action manifests itself as one-off gestures and mere signals of discontent to a distant offender. T-shirts, wristbands, bumper stickers, tweets, likes, follows, hashtags, concerts, songs, television shows, viral videos, avatars, memes, op-eds, blogs, sports, comedy, and video games. Individuals engage in these sorts of practices because they are fun and social. They are standard leisure time activities and typical expressions of personal identity: Who I am is defined by clothing I wear, activities I partake in, information I consume, and details about myself I choose to share with others. The appearance of engagement on behalf of human suffering is more important than actual engagement. Representing one's self as concerned with the welfare of others, particularly those in a far-off land, suffices for compassion and replaces the compulsion to act with personal satisfaction and contentment. Nobody ever actually has to do anything, as long as we all look good not doing it and feel pleased once it's not done. Performances over practices. Optics over antics.

Folding human rights into self-gratifying entertainment favors participation that serves the self, rather than the stated recipient, the global other. The tension between self-seeking and other-regarding action captures an essential dialectic of the current age: As capitalism penetrates through societies and deepens within cultures, attendant ideologies infiltrate, colonize, and reproduce modes of existence in their own image. These forces are in turn shaped by individual preferences, even those that include social consciousness and moral expression, thus producing personalized economies that bear the imprint of global capital filtered through a prism of popular sentimentality. A circumscribed belief system imposes meaning on the pursuit of pure self-interest in a supposedly value-free marketplace. When consumers interact with commerce in post-industrial neoliberal capitalism, they take part in shaping the terms. Economic exchange must feel a certain way to the consumer and must comply with a set of engrained ideals that express conscience. The personal is commercial and the commercial is personal—but neither is political, which is exactly how we like it.

Civic significance infects mass consumption, and monetary transaction propagates as political engagement. Advocacy practices channel commercial behavior in the service of human rights, leveraging awareness of suffering and injustice contextualized in the grocery store and shopping mall. Acts that wave limply in the direction of social change posit global citizens as consumers without interrupting business as usual. Fleeting, shallow expressions of ethical desire offer a major platform for advocacy groups to champion their causes while reaching individuals in a comfortable space. The mass appeal of human rights fosters a hybrid: Political demands for the rights and dignity of others articulated as inconsequential choices made in the moral marketplace.

The marriage between humanism and consumerism goes beyond its appearance in human rights advocacy. Commodities emblazoned with seals guaranteeing ethical chastity flood the shelves and aisles: fair trade, green, conflict free, and dolphin safe. Purchasing goods labeled as such does nothing to address the extraction of surplus value from labor, impending ecological collapse, or systemic roots of violence, though. In fact, these labels reinforce and retrench world-historical crimes. Consumerism actively obscures its negative effects on the world and the self. NGOs and coalitions that craft these strategies gain public traction for their issues, although thinly, making this dynamic mutually beneficial: Consumers feel better about their spending habits, and advocates skim resources for their operations. Participating in this charade requires compartmentalizing the origins of problems and any obligation to actually dispatch an appropriate solution. These modes of practice are innately apolitical and perhaps anti-political, inhibiting opportunities for deep and sustained involvement aimed at comprehensive problem solving.

Whatever critique we may want to muster, this is not a defective system. It is a feature of the design, not a bug. Indeed, this arrangement approximates the level of interest and dedication among the mass public and meets people where they are rather than challenging them to think or act otherwise. We willfully and joyfully enter into this bargain because it is fundamentally a good deal: I extend a meager hand to suffering strangers at no great cost to my own well-being and feel proud of my altruism while remaining confident in my status among the Western, Northern, intercontinental one-percent. I enjoy my secure, comfortable life and am rarely forced to confront human misery. Conscious consumption insulates and isolates consumers from the ills of the system that we so enjoy.

Self-delusion about the impact of global capitalism does not change the facts, though, from which it is increasingly more difficult to hide: outsourcing, race to the bottom, widening wealth gap, corporate malfeasance, oil spills, carbon emissions, global warming, housing crisis, recession, speculation, bailout, austerity, wage theft, slavery, human trafficking, student loan debt, social immobility, and rampant exploitation of scarce and treasured natural resources. Instead of investigating the consumer's role in any of these catastrophes or pointing to the adjustments that would be required to correct them, capitalism parades a civilized personality and a reformed version of itself. Responsible neighbor and citizen, corporate consumer capitalism softens the guilt and unease of affluence by directing this impulse toward charitable acts that distract from personal culpability and serve as a release valve for capitalism's most infamous evils. Personalized economies contain the imprint of an era in which the wealthy justify their excesses in terms of social good: "a portion of the proceeds" always seems to go toward some noble cause.

Maybe this argument is nothing more than the high-minded navel-gazing of a purist off floating in the ether, detached from reality, refusing to recognize the practical world. We must not to be naïve about the social practice of human rights: NGOs compete for resources and attention, and contend with a media context replete with scandal, drama, and spectacle. Organizations must go to all types of outrageous lengths to bring in money to support their operating expenses and raise their public profile. Whether or not we like it, marketing and posturing are central components to twenty-first-century human rights advocacy. Without them, all the "real" human rights work is for nothing. If a hard-hitting research report gathers dust in a file cabinet in a basement office somewhere, it is certain to have no influence. Given the long odds for any advocacy strategy to be effective, NGOs must have a full arsenal at their disposal to get their name and their work out in front of people. Perhaps even the most ridiculous, most obscene celebrity is better than no celebrity at all. Maybe Paris Hilton is a perfectly appropriate spokesperson because her media prowess certainly outweighs that of Mr. Wiesel; after all, "One Night in Paris" gets more hits than *Night*.

However, this purist rejects the notion that human rights advocacy must choose between form and content, between the substance of the work and expression with which it is presented to the world. NGOs are too often driven by their tactics, tempted by expediency to utilize devices that become monotonous responses to instrumental needs. Furthermore, it is imperative that NGOs begin to rethink their cultural imprint for the way it shapes their practices. While some observers have begun to write-off the human rights community as having peaked, I suggest that there is no more appropriate moment to engage in self-reflection and constructive critique than right now. Human rights is no panacea and does not offer solutions to all global problems. Human rights has no monopoly on social justice claims, and there are many examples of brutality and humiliation that human rights cannot adequately address. Recognizing its strengths in the context of its apparent limits can serve as the basis for a reinvigorated movement, reawakened as a hopeful embodiment of deep human aspirations.

Protecting human dignity is not simple business. It requires everyday egoists to think outside of themselves and consider the welfare of others. But more so, it demands recognizing the structural dimensions of suffering, of which consumers are a key component, whether or not any of us would like to admit it. By participating in mass consumption, we reproduce patterns of oppression and violence linked to global capitalism and the geopolitics by which the system is underwritten. An acute blind spot obstructs our view of this world-historic car crash. But, at the very moment that this contradiction is exposed as such, a transformation may occur to truly threaten status quo order and open space for a profoundly emancipatory politics. Human rights contains the potential to carry this vision forward, as an heir to radical internationalisms of the past, but only if we bring to light the sources of this myopia and focus attention on pragmatic next steps.

We damage our chances for success when we sell human rights with shortcuts. Asking for small investments only begets small returns. Big change requires big action. The twenty-first-century human rights advocacy community actually thinks that catastrophic problems can be tackled with meager acts, that we can literally change the world without leaving our couch, that our comfort is somehow disconnected from the suffering of others. This approach to politics assumes individuals are lazy and uncritical, unable to understand complex dynamics and unwilling to mobilize in the service of real solutions. I do not believe this is true. Vast publics continually express a desire to be engaged, only to be met with insignificant requests. We are the human rights movement that we foster. And by critically investigating the origins and impact of these phenomena, we can determine where Paris Hilton came from, what she is doing here, and how we can do better.

CHAPTER 2

Mass Appeals for the Rights of Others

International human rights live in the hearts of advocates but are not native. The ideas that constitute human rights are born of struggle and catastrophe, and through agitation emerge institutionalized in official documents. Human rights travel from declarations and conventions into the conscience of ordinary people on a nonlinear path guided by translators and funneled through filters. Nongovernmental organizations serve primary functions as conduits for the diffusion of human rights as they seek to cultivate audiences of support. Strategic communication efforts toward recruitment, fund-raising, and mobilization target average individuals for engagement on human rights issues. NGOs interpret human rights for the uninitiated public, by defining what they are, explaining their origins and rationales, describing how they apply, and outlining potential responses to abuse. But a profound subtext of cues is also transmitted through NGO messaging pertaining to crucial social, cultural, and psychological dimensions of human rights engagement. Fostering a constituency for the defense of human dignity entails shaping how average folks think and feel about their relationship to international life, connection to universal norms, and commitment to matters outside of themselves.

In the final quarter of the twentieth century, saving the world became a cool and convenient thing to do. No longer confined to the hobbies of hippies around a campfire, the actions of the black bloc at the barricades, or the professional dictates of elite lawyers, rights-based articulations of dignity and justice are now pervasive features of the Western perspective.

J. R. Pruce, *The Mass Appeal of Human Rights*, Human Rights Interventions, https://doi.org/10.1007/978-3-319-92075-7_2

Human rights principles grace the lips of celebrities at charity events and provoke the television audience to question its obligations to distant suffering. NGOs brand themselves with carefully crafted logos and focus-grouped slogans, while relying on social media "likes" as micro-testimonials that ambiguously attest to their relevance. Speaking in rights-talk is normal parlance when it once was not—and more than normal, human rights is an accepted, attractive, and approachable framework for concerns about deprivation and violence. The cultural currency of human rights permits an opening for individuals to become involved without the risk of being socially ostracized as troublemakers or extremists.

When human rights broke through in the mid-1970s, it constituted a transformation not only in global politics but also in everyday affairs (Cmiel 1999; Eckel and Moyn 2013). A rapidly expanding NGO sector incited and leveraged notions of identification with the vulnerable other that peaked during episodes of great emergency. Ordinary people confronted news of human despair by conveying a significant capacity for concern during ritualized crisis events. As a moral symptom of globalization, and a by-product of shifting economic currents and advances in information technology, an ethos of compassion developed among the audience containing a striking communalist and egalitarian spirit, at least in its rhetoric; consider, as I do in this chapter, the meaning expressed in the song "We Are the World," a sweet and gentle manifestation of humanistic empathy. The rise of human rights as a mainstream cause tracks precisely to its integration with elements of popular culture, particularly at moments of profound shock in global politics: famine, war, genocide, and mass atrocities. Citizen participation in world politics presents plausible evidence for the prospects of developing a collective response to conflict based on cosmopolitanism and solidarity, in which national borders or private interests matter little and the protection of human welfare rises to universal concern. Support for human rights advocacy gained traction as a conventional social cause by providing a set of principles with which average people mediate the chaotic world and explore their role in it.

This shift did not occur spontaneously or by accident. A host of principal actors and architects deliberately cultivated a relationship between Western publics and the embryonic human rights community. However, terms of this relationship from its dawn over fifty years ago have consistently relied upon features of consumer capitalism to draw in, engage, and retain supporters. Despite its usefulness, though, consumerism immanently affects and inherently limits the tactical interventions and strategic efforts of human rights. Stories contained in the chapters that follow focus not only on the use of media and culture in advocacy campaigns but also on how media and culture are fundamentally shaped by capitalism, which subsequently influences advocacy. For instance, that seeing suffering on television fails to ignite a sustainable human rights response requires understanding broadcast media and visual culture as they are situated within political and economic structures (see Chapter 3). It is essential to identify communicative spaces as sites of contestation over meaning and, therefore, power. Media and culture are not neutral categories and as such must be critically investigated.

For human rights, this orientation compels an analysis of the ways organizations and coalitions utilize media and culture to build strength. Assessing the impact of outreach strategies on the community demands, we look into the effect of capitalism's forces on the form and content of human rights practice. In terms of form, we must consider the social bonds that connect advocates and establish the movement as a collectivity of individuals working together in common cause. As well, form includes the aesthetic qualities of NGO campaigns and the projected identities that express how they wish to be perceived by their target audiences. With regard to content, I focus on the articulation of human rights claims by advocates, how causal arguments are made, and what solutions are proposed. Consumer capitalism works to preserve a status quo that human rights seeks to disrupt by reprioritizing the centrality of fairness and decency in public decision making. This tension is a central driver of the arguments in the book.

Human rights, in law and theory, imagines a world that defies expropriation, unseats patriarchy, and combats bigotry. Human rights justifies the self-determination of individuals and groups and provides a blueprint for the free development of human capabilities. The human rights project is indeed utopian and aspirational, even if it is politically unrealized. Neoliberal capitalism, conversely, insists on inequality, exploitation, and domination, pitting the system squarely at odds with a robust vision of a rights-protecting society. The human rights framework provides societies with the tools to resist and repel the smooth operation of capitalist accumulation and the political arrangements that facilitate it. Therefore, when human rights organizations deploy mechanisms of mass consumption, attempts to check power and raise-up the marginalized can at best only provide temporary fixes. Structures stay in place. Power retains license to operate with bare constraints. Human dignity remains precarious, and human rights prove to be ill equipped to carry the hopes of their champions across the finish line.

However, this is not an innate quality of the human rights idea, nor is it essential or predetermined. Critical studies address the question of how we understand the perceived weaknesses of human rights. Human rights emerged as a palatable moral alternative to polarized cold war politics, appealing to disenchanted liberals, not radicals, and was never intended to cause much of a stir (Hopgood 2006; Moyn 2010). But, as a socially constructed discourse, human rights are malleable, subject to struggles over meaning, and may be used to dominate as well as liberate (Perugini and Gordon 2015). Contemporary human rights began as a middling enterprise anchored to no ideology in particular, making it entirely susceptible to manipulation. Or, perhaps more nefariously, this apolitical posture masks the invisible way in which human rights discourse exercises power and takes up space in the moral and political landscape (Brown 2004). The mainstream appeal of human rights, impressed upon it through mass advocacy campaigns, is a construct and not a natural or inherent quality. Another phase in the life of this movement is as likely to be around the next corner as it is to end tomorrow.

This is not an exercise in rose-colored revisionism that wishes to return to a golden era of human rights that was once radical and solidaritistic, but has been reduced to an orgy of impotent, silly self-seeking. Instead, the narrative lays out an historic unfolding of a new era of human rights tracked against deepening ties between the global and the grassroots. Political, cultural, and social spaces stretch from the international to the individual. Institutions expand, NGOs proliferate, and human rights ideas seep and drip down into the lives of normal people. Constructing human rights "from below" in this sense is different from considering the impact of social movements on global norms (Falk 2009; Stammers 2009). Instead, the "from below" perspective here highlights the impact of audience's associations on the constitution of human rights advocacy. The communicative practices of human rights organizations shape public engagement, which in turn sharply influences our shared understanding of human rights. Critically detailing the terms of this evolution demands recognizing the remarkable transformation brought on by globalization, as well as acknowledging the missed moments and squandered opportunities for what *did not* happen over this span.

The connective tissue linking ordinary people to international human rights cultivates specific affiliations for supporters and facilitates any attempt at movement-building. Not only are the social relations that constitute human rights networks underexplored, but they also present a crucial site of human rights practice worthy of our attention. Contemporary advocacy relies on mass mobilization to provide credibility to NGO demands, yet the composition of this broad base has never been scrutinized. Researchers pour over United Nations transcripts, dissect foreign policy signals, and count references to NGO reports in global media. Yet, in many respects, the power and authority of human rights derive from the ability to call upon a constituency of support, a variable or criterion that is difficult to identify for it does not exist in any tangible place. For instance, the core method of "naming and shaming" relies on faith in the audience's reception to the publicity of abuse. But what informs this reception? Human rights must mean something in public if the politics of information is going to be usefully deployed. For this reason, investigating the global public's bonds with human rights norms creates new opportunity to comprehend the salience of human rights demands in international relations.

This opening chapter outlines the terms and tools with which I embark on this critical examination of the human rights community. The first section locates human rights advocacy on the terrain of public engagement in an era of globalized mass consumption. In the second section, I situate the current project in dialogue with a slate of research in critical human rights studies, much of which seeks to address similar observations but leaves notable and persistent gaps. The final section details the Critical Theory framework that informs my analysis. Drawing heavily on the Frankfurt School permits a rigorous approach that emphasizes the deleterious influence of consumer capitalism on political action and explains the negative impact commercialism has on challenges to power. Profound potential exists for human rights to take shape as the basis for a transnational grassroots movement and only clear-eyed, hard-nosed introspection has the capacity to prompt the kind of radical break that is necessary.

The Work of Angels, Advocates, and Activists

If women and men were angels, no nongovernmental organizations would be necessary. But we are not, and neither are our politicians, military officers, or corporate executives. NGOs strenuously strive to conjure and extract the saintliness from our hearts to put to use in defense of humanity. Our capacity to care for others is commonly depicted nesting within co-centric circles spiraling outward, with the concerned individual in the middle and the suffering others situated on the outer rings, the furthest of which receiving the least attention (Singer 2011). "We are human beings and not altruism machines...we empathize more readily with people who more closely resemble us and are near" (Rieff 2003, 7). Average people are not predisposed to give of themselves completely for the sake of less fortunate others. It is not clear if this is morally obligatory or even a reasonable expectation (Singer 1972). Even if proximity to suffering was not a factor, we don't do a very good job of caring for those nearby, in our own communities and cities, making the phenomenon of global citizen engagement that much more confounding.

Despite not being hardwired for caring at a distance, this sentiment is a central feature of the world in which we live and a product of cause-marketing campaigns and intentional communication efforts (Richey and Ponte 2011). Opportunities for global citizen engagement appear at the check-out aisle of the grocery store and on the price tags of retail items at the mall. Caring is a component of celebrity identity, and specialist firms can be hired to determine which cause most appropriately complements a celebrity's persona (Winston 2017). Whether we focus concern on issues related to the environment, food, animals, labor, trade, or poverty, the seals of approval stamped on our products guide us through our ethical decision making. Telethons and infomercials solicit for our donation dollars with evocative messages and sad imagery. Petitions for signatures circulate freely online and persist on the clipboards of summer interns patrolling busy street corners. Social causes are woven into the backdrop of modern life.

Manufacturing compassion commodifies concern as organizations compete in the marketplace for the attention of the audience. Audience members, in turn, select how and where to dedicate this scarce resource. The calculus driving this choice suggests various possible inputs: Who/what is the object of concern? Why are they in need of assistance or support? What is being asked of us? Will my contribution actually help? Considering these sorts of questions requires that we parse the causes that are presented to us because they are not all equal. Issues are distinguished by the work that organizations do and the expectations they have of their supporters, and these criteria then shape the outreach methods and the demands of mobilization. Not all global causes are appropriately labeled "humanitarian," simply because they rely on some baseline conception of humanity. Humanitarianism is a specific field of practice and of law, not a catchall for things that make us feel warm inside. Humanism is insufficient because it is too broad, even if it captures something general about a particular moral disposition. Conceptual and empirical mistakes are made when fields as distinct as human rights and humanitarianism are conflated, collapsing into a mélange of do-gooderism.

Human rights advocacy is a unique mode of global citizen engagement and demands explicit definition. Human rights advocacy is the practice of promoting the rights of others, guided by the internationally recognized framework of norms designed to support and protect human dignity. In common parlance, to advocate is to support or recommend or to speak on behalf of an issue or a person. An advocate is the actor who performs this role (consider, for instance, a legal advocate). "Advocacy" refers to the practice itself, and the term captures a central programmatic and ordered quality essential to our comprehension of the subject. Advocacy occurs across the ideological spectrum and in wide-ranging issue areas including the environment, animal welfare, firearms, food, and innumerable others. Advocacy is not a random occurrence or standalone act, but an institutionalized, systematized, and habituated performance. On the global level (although this is certainly true domestically too), a well-developed and growing sector of actors participates in advocacy and shapes its work and the way it is perceived by the international community.

To understand advocacy this way, I believe, corresponds to the way the word is used in ordinary language, as well as the way it is used by scholars of human rights. In their seminal study of these issues, Margaret Keck and Kathryn Sikkink operate with this assumption but fail to problematize it all when they plainly write, "advocates plead the cause of others or defend a cause or a population" (1998, 9). The very constitution of transnational advocacy networks hinges on representation of one group by another. We commonly speak of human rights advocates as those who advocate for the *cause* of human rights, but advocates are ultimately concerned with the human beings whose dignity constitutes the "cause." Excluding the human object of human rights advocacy ignores a key dimension that differentiates this act from that which addresses animal welfare or ecological degradation. Foregrounding the human object of human rights advocacy draws crucial attention to the ethical considerations that should guide the practice and failing to do so creates space for dehumanizing errors.

Lastly, human rights advocacy contains an inherent connection to transnational action. The relationship between the Western advocate-subject and non-Western victim-object is shaped by distance, and fraught with complex power disparities. That advocates opt to engage in human rights issues in another country—often instead and at the expense of local struggles—says a great deal about the politics of human rights. Transnationality raises pervasive questions about what a truly global, truly grassroots human rights movement would look like. When we talk about human rights advocacy, we talk about a patterned practice, structured around a community of professional organizations and networks that engage in rights-based campaigns to protect the dignity of other people. Often human rights advocacy relies on mass appeal to generate broad support for campaign work, but this is not a prerequisite or definitional.

When groups of ordinary people act as their own advocates we do not call it advocacy per se; instead, we generally employ a unique term with its own history and cultural associations. *Activism* is distinct from advocacy in that, as a practice, it articulates charges against an instrument of power directly by those affected, without proxy. The absence of an intermediary is an essential difference between advocacy and activism. Colonial histories and persistent inequalities inject suspicion into relationships constituted and justified by acting for the benefit of others. Goodwill and noble intentions do not go far enough to overcome the political obstacles presented by interlocutors in this sensitive area. Human rights advocates are conscious of their vulnerability to accusation and, influenced by humanitarianism, assume an apolitical persona. Distancing themselves from politics, advocates defend their interventions as expressive of the universal values that underwrite human rights norms. This articulation permits an opening for advocates to engage on "policy changes that cannot be easily linked to a rationalist understanding of their 'interests'" (Keck and Sikkink 1998, 9). Activism, on the other hand, sidesteps accusations of paternalism altogether as activists assert their own claims and pursue their own interests, often in the face of great risk to their physical security. Delineating among these practices provides a basis for theorizing about the role of subject and object in human rights advocacy.

Taking a "social practice" approach to the study of human rights advocacy demands looking not only at the efforts and interventions of practitioners, but also at the way human rights are constructed and conveyed from NGOs to target audiences (Pruce 2015). Mass appeals for human rights serve a key function as crucial sites of meaning and interpretation. What do human rights mean to ordinary people? What is the public's association with human rights and how does that influence the receptivity of advocacy campaigns? How do ingrained, historically and culturally derived associations in turn generate certain types of advocacy messaging? Do we think of human rights advocacy as a means of pursuing "personal fulfillment," "maintaining the social order," or "radical change"? (De Waal 2015, 25). The psychic dimension—intellectual, emotional, and cognitive—of human rights is an inescapable ingredient that informs how norms are promoted. When human rights materialize in mass media and pop culture productions, they function to fundamentally translate and define human rights for a lay cross section of global citizens. Examining this process, its strengths and its flaws, provides an opportunity to fill in the gaps in contemporary critiques of human rights.

Tough Love for Human Rights

Human rights seems to have a target on its back lately, with a spate of academic critique aimed at bringing the community back to earth. This is not unreasonable, unfair, or unanticipated. The meteoric rise of human rights into mainstream consciousness was bound to attract suspicion from observers opposed to the project outright, as well as those inclined toward sympathy. For the most part, the trend in critical human rights studies is situated in the latter category as constructive self-reflection drives thinkers to pause and reconsider. Tough love requires we recognize that the community can do better, if only its supporters train a skeptical lens on the operations of advocates and defenders. Communities are largely insular and defensive units, sealed off from introspection and resistant to change and the human rights community is no different, which is why critiques of human rights are often derided or dismissed as efforts to undermine the program (Pruce 2015). However, immanent critique is not about making human rights weaker, but stronger. In this section, I engage with three strands of critique that capture persistent and striking questions facing human rights and fundamentally compel this book's line of inquiry.

What Explains the Apolitical Nature of Transnational Human Rights Advocacy?

Humanitarianism is apolitical: neutrality and impartiality permit NGOs access to conflict-affected regions. Were humanitarian NGOs to call out abusive states, they would likely be denied safe passage to the suffering individuals they serve. Human rights, on the other hand, have a more complex relationship to politics, and the community's apolitical stances are increasingly difficult to comprehend and justify.

Human rights on their face are deeply political for the assertion that positive domestic law must be adopted to protect the dignity and autonomy of all human beings. Since legislative processes are political processes, as are demands for accountability or transparency, clearly matters of interest and power factor into human rights claims. This is true of human rights activism and perhaps even more so of human rights advocacy. If a stakeholder in a society makes demands of her own government, there is a rational expectation of being heard even if only to be denied. Citizens share privileged roles, sometimes codified as rights, and if an individual or group is facing persecution, citizens direct claims at their state.

Yet, when a global citizen makes a human rights claim in a country that she is not a resident or national of, political tension is heightened. Where does anyone get the nerve to criticize the domestic affairs of a state of which she is not a citizen? On what grounds? It's a particularly galling intervention in the matters of a political community to which one does not belong. The state system is not necessarily designed to accommodate cross-border criticism of sovereigns by non-nationals; or at least sovereigns have no natural reason to abide. But this is changing too. In these terms, transnational human rights advocacy should be understood as a practice that confronts the exercise of power in another country, which cannot be anything other than a political demand.

But this is not the position adopted by human rights NGOs, neither in principle nor in practice. Instead of emphasizing the profoundly political dimensions of human rights, advocacy organizations avoid them by framing their work in universal, cosmopolitan, internationalist moral terms: All people's rights are all of our concern, regardless of our origins or identity. One intentional feature of this application is the appeal to morality and moral supremacy. The terms of the debate are situated starkly: Either you protect particular powerful interests or you represent the rights of all. Given this framework, supporters can make tidy arguments about participating in ethical behavior without getting messy in the details of policy reform or domestic governance. Samuel Moyn argues that the relationship between morality on the one hand and politics on the other, in the context of human rights advocacy, was shaped by the polarized waning years of the cold war period. "This was to be a recipe of tremendous power: in the face of soiled utopias in politics, a nonpartisan morality existed outside and above them" (2010, 132). This environment generated NGOs that sidestep the genuinely political nature of advocacy in favor of the appearance that human rights shares humanitarianism's neutral qualities.

A deliberate turn away from ideological movements of the era, human rights appealed to global citizens starved for a new vision. "It transferred the aspiration to purity once associated with revolutionary ardor to the less totalistic program of human rights. Human rights were preferable because they were strategically necessary and practically feasible, but also because they were morally pure" (Moyn 2010, 170–71). Advocates are not asked to take a blood oath about what system of government was best or how to most effectively distribute economic goods. Human rights was not a commitment on that scale. Hardly a robust program, human rights meant to tinker at the edges of the system, proposing incremental ways to protect the vulnerable. Moyn stresses that these elements—moralism and minimalism—are the core strengths of human rights.

Over time, though, human rights organizations expanded their mandates and took on issues such as economic rights that demand a structural perspective when human rights is not equipped to offer one.[1] The apolitical posture remained as the demands on human rights advocacy intensified. This shift from moral purity and minimalism to maximal political enterprise is why Moyn believes the utopian currency of human rights is in decline because it cannot bear the weight of its own expectations. However, moralism may be the true shackle. As human rights shifted to a political agenda, its advocates continued to express antipolitics. The human rights movement's dilemma is not in its shift to politics, but in its devotion to an apolitical moralism.

Human rights is not a substantive moral theory, only meekly outlining assumptions about political, social, cultural, and economic life. What occupies the actual substance of these areas should be determined through democratic practices in accordance with local ideals. This conception of human rights avoids judgment and prioritizes tolerance and diversity of opinion. Even staunch universalists will concede that some discrepancy in implementation must be expected and permitted; no defender of human rights will readily admit that all states can and should have identical systems for law or welfare provision. Taking no position on form of government, means of market exchange, or reading of scripture, for instance, the human rights community projects a vision that deliberately positions itself as catchall, able to encompass multiple and even conflicting claims of injustice and insecurity.

Emergent manifestations of human rights maintain a safe distance from politics as such. Human rights norms are said to be apolitical in that they do not correlate with any partisan stance or philosophical persuasion. Human rights standards are above politics. Human rights operate outside of partiality and bias, on a plane apart from the Left to Right spectrum. Because the values human rights express apply to all human beings, no petty parochial matter may be permitted to obstruct their realization. NGOs advance this argument by claiming to speak for all, as an objective third party.

Borrowing heavily from humanitarian dogma, human rights advocates take shelter behind universalism so as to maximize access and impact without committing themselves to specific policy prescriptions. They suggest that human rights protection need not threaten social order or undermine traditional hierarchies. Human rights accommodation conducted within the context of existing structures may involve significant institutional reform but avoids major upheaval or disruption; or so the argument goes. However, in the process of positing a vernacular of rights that appeals to everyone, its champions expose the soul of the enterprise to manipulation.

Rooted in nothing-in-particular, aside from thin moral claims, the clarion call of human rights travels fluidly between groups and movements. All claiming ownership, human rights are talking points for both liberals and conservatives. Dictators and dissidents each articulate their goals in rights language, and each believes theirs is the proper and authoritative interpretation. Multinational corporations embed the human rights agenda into their platforms on social responsibility and good global citizenship. Rogue states hijack the United Nations Human Rights Council. Are these only expressions of clever maneuvering, opportunism, and flawed institutional design, or is something more fundamental happening? Can anyone claim to own human rights discourse and challenge its use by hostile actors? Is there no baseline for assessing and calling out hypocrisy? Would this even be desirable if it were possible? Who are the gatekeepers of human rights principles if not transnational NGOs? Advocates worked tirelessly to integrate human rights into mainstream discussions of global politics, but in articulating a palatable and apolitical version of human rights, the product has become diluted, weak, and adrift.

Though, to gain a grasp of precisely why human rights takes shape as a rootless project, an additional layer of theoretical depth is necessary. Appealing to morality over politics as basis for the movement has had implications for human rights practice, specifically in terms of outreach and communication, for it directly influences the tenor of messaging and the expectations of the audience. This notion that human rights is apolitical has been transmitted to and internalized by masses of supporters who perpetuate the idea through their engagement in advocacy campaigns. Mass media and pop culture—and the system of consumer capitalism out of which they emerge—do crucial work by producing and reproducing the apolitical view and, therefore, must be central subjects of investigation. If the first step is to identify the origins of human rights as pure morality as Moyn did, the next step is to apply a lens that helps us make sense of its specific manifestations in human rights practice. Critical Theory, as outlined below, provides a compelling framework for conceptualizing why politics drop out of political movements and the role capitalism plays in this process.

What would it be like to rethink the adoption of moral purity as the underwriting force for human rights advocacy? What would it look like if human rights pivoted back toward the "revolutionary ardor" of historic rights-based movements? What if we are returning to an era that thirsts for a new grand narrative, a utopian reclamation of human rights? In addition to addressing the political tension within human rights advocacy, any revival of human rights must also consider the social composition of such a movement. Another recurring theme proposes a question about the contours and constitution of the contemporary human rights community.

Can Human Rights Be a Basis for Global Solidarity?

It is not clear that human rights is a movement at all. The nomenclature "human rights movement" is applied to capture the common cause and shared discourse that unites organizations claiming the mantle of human rights, but how far we choose to push the label reflects editorial preference. That, in this sense, human rights is a transnational project stretches traditional understandings of what a movement is, and is clearly more aspirational than it is descriptive. That primary units of this "movement" are organizations, not individuals, also presents an obstacle to easily grouping human rights as such with typical social movement examples; this facet makes it all the more necessary to understand the relationship between individuals, organizations, and "the movement." But maybe these features still do not disqualify designating human rights as a movement. At least, it is fair to say that the transnational human rights movement, if it is a movement, is unlike anything the world has seen before.

Scholars of social movements and political sociology help provide context for this assessment. Typically, when social movement organizations (SMOs) form, they emerge out of grassroots movements in an effort to consolidate gains and advance their cause to the next level. SMOs prove to be effective in mobilizing resources through formal channels, as well as legitimizing claims of marginalized populations (McCarthy and Zald 1977). However, as Frances Fox Piven and Richard Cloward argue, the organizational form of a social movement limits spontaneity and "enforce[s] political docility" and, for these reasons, are ineffective in exacting concessions from the state (1979, 7 and throughout). The transition from protest to advocacy leads the movement down a path of moderation and timidity. "Organizations endure, in short, by abandoning their oppositional politics" (Piven and Cloward 1979, xxi). In regulatory and bureaucratic terms, when SMOs file as nonprofit organizations, they are "required to shape their goals to be more in line with what is defined by the state as charitable ends, are prohibited from engaging in certain forms of resource aggregation and political advocacy and are more conservative in their tactical repertoires" (Cress 1997, 344). SMOs willingly file for nonprofit status seemingly aware of the trade-off between the political powers of direct action from below in exchange for tax incentives.

The tension between movements and organizations is reflected as well in the strategies they employ. "Protest organizations use outsider tactics or disruptive means—such as sit-ins, die-ins, and marches—to influence policies, public officials, or public opinion. Advocacy groups use routine means like lobbying and litigation to influence policies and public opinion in a variety of institutional settings" (Minkoff 1999, 1668). Thinking about the human rights community in these terms provides tools with which to evaluate how it is situated on the fault line between movements and organizations. Unlike traditional SMOs, the "global human rights movement" is not a progressive iteration of a social movement; it is a community of organizations, not an aggregation of grassroots protest movements, not in the literal sense. Critics of human rights may wish it were otherwise but comparing a transnational NGO against the standards of a strong local social movement makes little sense. We can hold NGOs accountable for being elitist and detached from the ground, but that is central to their design, not a deficiency.

Along these lines, Stephen Hopgood subtly posits an ideal for a global human rights movement preferable to the bloated, self-aggrandizing network that, in his view, represents human rights today (2013). Hopgood critiques the human rights movement for not being a better, more authentic social movement. Nowhere does he explicitly articulate what a model movement should be, but Hopgood surely goes to some lengths to describe what it should not be. Through parsing his objections to contemporary human rights and by sorting tidbits of suggestion, it becomes clearer what he means.

The closest approximation, and a reference that Hopgood draws upon, is Malcolm Gladwell's essay on the Save Darfur Coalition, which is unsuccessful because it relies on weak ties (Gladwell 2010). Citing sociologist Mark Granovetter (1973), Gladwell proposes that the effectiveness of the American civil rights movement was due to the social connections between activists, who knew each other outside the movement and built community and solidarity based on those relationships. Save Darfur, on the other hand, relied on strangers to act together, largely online rather than in real life, at a great distance to the space they wished to affect. Firstly, it is intensely problematic to compare Save Darfur to civil rights for many reasons. They bear almost nothing in common, aside from a marginal overlap in the area of "rights." The former struggled for the rights of others (advocacy), while the latter put their bodies on the line for their own rights and dignity (activism). It would be very nice if transnational networks were constituted by people with close ties to one another, but placing this impossible expectation on the human rights community is unreasonable. If there is anything we can learn from this juxtaposition, transnational advocacy movements are more complex than national or local social movements and more difficult to build and execute.

Following Gladwell, Hopgood swipes at "slacktivism" in the process of detailing all that is wrong with human rights today. Slacktivism is activism for slackers, which is to say a form of public engagement that does not ask or expect much of its supporters. Usually tied to digital media and social networks, slacktivism is a pejorative term that paints its participants as lazy, selfish gawkers who pretend to care about things, but not enough to do anything about it. Civil rights activists who sat-in at lunch counters in South Carolina risked physical harm for the issues that mattered to them. Signatories to an online petition or recipients of Save Darfur listserv e-mails sacrifice nothing. Privileging direct action over indirect gesture, criticism of slacktivists imagines a richer form of engagement emerging in which these people could be transformed into activists.

Critics assume that lazy people can grow into non-lazy people if only they were sprinkled with magic movement dust. Sometimes this takes shape as a technophobic throwback that blames the opportunity to be slacktivists on the digital platforms themselves: If it weren't for the Internet, all of these engaged citizens would be out of their houses, in the streets, protesting instead. Of the fallacies driving the most ordinary versions of this critique, one assumes that slacktivists could be converted to activists, if only the messaging were right. Another insists that slacktivism fails to produce social goods because of its low-risk, low-reward nature. Research suggests, in fact, that much maligned forms of viral engagement are incredibly useful in raising money which indeed produces social benefit for medical research, for instance (Fawzy 2016). As well, there is actually a conversion rate from online behavior, such as likes and tweets, into more active expressions of support for causes (Conroy et al. 2012; Park 2013). Human rights certainly trafficks in slacktivism but the extent to which advocacy is structurally dependent on it remains dubious; often feeling like an overplayed hand. It is, though, a strong tactical example of how global human rights is profoundly unlike traditional social movements.

Hopgood's core critique rests on the fact that transnational human rights advocacy revolving around major NGOs lacks the essential properties of strongly bonded, local, grassroots movements. While this is not a shocking admission, the differences matter. "In local and solidarity-based rights activism an individual benefits in principle from collective success and builds up a store of good-will for future interactions" (Hopgood 2013, 107). Movements constructed around "reciprocity relations," in which, presumably, activists build power through the strength of their obligations to one another is somehow better or more preferable than a "protest of strangers" (Hopgood 2013, 107). Hopgood asks, "Who are these people, what do they believe in, what are they really like, and how accountable are they for their decisions? They have only mob authority. This may be the best we can hope for, but it is not sustained or sustainable ethical commitment" (Hopgood 2013, 107). This last assertion, that "sustainable ethical commitment" is the true prize is key to understanding the absence that Hopgood observes when he looks at the universe of human rights advocacy.

He continues, "When activism is consumption, the audience is a 'flash mob' who move quickly on to the next big thing. Their interests are not engaged, and they do not generate any political or social capital, all of which denies them a sustained voice" (Hopgood 2013, 108). Hopgood rightly points out that citizen participation in advocacy campaigns is a fleeting series of one-offs, lurching from crisis to crisis, failing to develop a standing constituency of advocates to call upon when trouble erupts. The early decades of Amnesty International demonstrate that movement-building was in fact a high priority, but the pressures of growth and transformation eclipsed this core objective. "Global, hierarchical organizations are the antithesis of such collective action—they stifle diversity and discipline dissent," echoing Piven and Cloward (Hopgood 2013, 114–15). Amnesty International often calls itself a movement, as do other NGOs, but defining what the *global human rights movement* is, in a singular coherent sense, remains obscure.

If we were to look for historical examples of "sustainable ethical commitment" to transnational human rights issues, the Anti-Apartheid Movement looms largest likely because it is the only such example that anyone alive has witnessed or personally participated in. It also was long-standing, running for nearly forty years, and unusually successful. The movement claimed supporters ranging from schoolchildren to celebrities and utilized a multifaceted tactical approach that included boycott and divestment, as well as direct action and protest. South African racist crimes were clear and the justice of the cause unquestionable. The movement consisted of a transnational network of NGOs working in partnership with grassroots activists, whose lives were threatened daily by the white government. From the standpoint of solidarity and sustainability, the Anti-Apartheid Movement is an ideal model for human rights. But replicating the model across a broad set of human rights issues, rather than a discrete circumstance, may be impossible, which should make us reconsider whether we learn the correct lessons from this case at all.

Perugini and Gordon react to similar features of contemporary advocacy and remark on structure and strategy. Human Rights Watch (HRW), for instance, "explicitly rejects popular participation" favoring an elite, legalistic approach, which in turn "often negates and even subjugates certain forms of more radical politics" (Perugini and Gordon 2015, 130, 133). Practitioners "only rarely take to the streets in an attempt to occupy public spaces," evidencing the way human rights "lose their critical edge...[and] become nonthreatening to structures of domination..." (Perugini and Gordon 2015, 135–36). Imagining the researchers and lawyers at HRW executing radical direct action campaigns is misplaced and odd, but the sentiment contained in these arguments posits further evidence of this trend among critical observers.

The failure of human rights to evolve into a grassroots solidarity movement is a consistent trope among critics. Although this is often subtext, rather overtly declared. It is as if the bureaucratic, professionalized, donor-chasing, attention seekers that we observe in transnational human rights NGOs have lost their truth, their authenticity, their grounding. The "purity of the struggle" is lost (Moyn 2010). Without truth and authenticity, human rights is no different than any other pursuit, which comes close to suggesting that either we discard the project or step aside and wait for it to spoil and wither. Is there an idea we can believe in that takes us out of ourselves and applies our inherent decency to a worthwhile cause? Where is our Anti-Apartheid Movement? Equal parts nostalgia and post-modern malaise, global human rights in theory possesses the apparatus to step into this void, but up until now has not dedicated its efforts to building a movement worthy of this legacy or these expectations. An element of romanticism also mixes in with critique—a romanticism that cringes to think that a noble enterprise like human rights must navigate the raunchy material world. This intersection with capitalism provides the final problematique.

What Role Does Consumerism Play in Shaping Human Rights?

When Hopgood describes activism as "consumption," he alludes to a materialist argument without committing to it, which is remarkably common in human rights critique. Perugini and Gordon criticize HRW for its annual budget exceeding $50 million and because its offices in the Empire State Building are "adjacent to corporations such as Walgreen, Bank of America, and LinkedIn," suggesting that this proximity infects the NGO's operations (2015, 130). It's a strange correlation, really, that being close to corporations may impact the way human rights organizations operate but thinking about capitalism as a contagion is not off base if justified in specific terms. Lilie Chouliaraki freely associates the weakness of post-humanitarian solidarity with processes of commodification and forces of neoliberalism, but openly refutes any debt to Marxist critique (2012). Sneering terms that refer to the advocacy sector as the "human rights industry" are frequently deployed by both the Left and the Right with endless abandon, yet with little gravity (Kovalik 2012; Delaney 2015; Hassan 2015; Henningsen 2016). Consumption, consumerism, and capitalism become symbolic dog whistles for critics preaching to the converted, rather than analytical categories with history, meaning, and power. Why do critics think capitalism corrupts human rights, yet resist deploying these terms in serious ways, in a full-throated materialist critique?

One need not be a revolutionary to be aware of the influence of capitalist culture on the conduct of NGOs and nonprofits. Beneath this discomfort is a lingering assumption that humanistic projects must remain righteous, which requires remaining a safe distance from the ugly face of capitalism. Money is dirty and human rights are pure. When they intersect in the manifestation of major NGOs, questions arise as to whether or not management can navigate these murky waters properly. Can the organization raise and spend funds in a manner consistent with mission? Can overheard expenditures such as labor costs be kept sufficiently low, in order to maximize impact of "real" work? Can the organization pursue strategies without chasing money, maintaining autonomy from philanthropists? Mixing in elite financial circles, with wealthy donors and bankrolled foundations, shines an unflattering light on the nonprofit world. Charging $500 per plate at gala dinners to benefit world hunger is not a good look.

Strident labels like "non-profit industrial complex" are applied to the NGO world to expose it and explode the myths of nobility and cleanliness (INCITE! Women of Color Against Violence 2009). Claiming that NGOs care less about solving problems than they do for keeping themselves employed and their friend's pockets lined is one example of an argument for how capitalism taints human rights. It shuffles our priorities, takes us out of the struggle, and pacifies the rebellious nature of our calling. Marketing the organization can also take on a life of its own and begin to appear as though propping up the NGO's image supersedes the cause itself (King 2006). Scrambling for the attention of donors and audiences creates a market in which NGOs compete against one another, compelling organizations to adapt in counterintuitive ways. Competition further distorts priorities even in the process of selecting the issues to work on (Bob 2002). Is the expectation that human rights organizations should pursue the worst suffering and the hardest cases, or those in which they can have the most impact, sometimes characterized as "low hanging fruit"? While this is not an either/or decision, introducing competition warps any attempt at idealistic reasoning. If human rights rests on moral purity, commercialization damages, perhaps fatally, any such claim. We expect human rights organizations to do impossible work without miring themselves in the material world—an impossibly high expectation. And yet, when observers critique the impact of commercialization on human rights, they decry the effect it has on human rights and even fault NGOs for pursuing these strategies, rather than issue broader assertions about the toxic nature of consumer capitalism as a system.

Lilie Chouliaraki is most notably guilty of this sin in her work on post-humanitarianism and, like Hopgood, only by dissecting and analyzing offset phrases can we determine some affirmative articulation of vision. Quoting one passage at length will illuminate the core of her subterranean argument:

> ...the utilitarian solidarity of post-humanitarianism, I contend next, reflects and reproduces a specifically *neoliberal* conception of humanitarianism that replaces conviction with consumption...but two specific features of neoliberalism are particularly relevant to post-humanitarianism: its *pragmatism*, which turns the communication of solidarity into artful story-telling, rather than also using it as a resource for judgement on the politics of vulnerability; and its *privatism*, which situates acts of solidarity within the private realm and aims at empowering consumers, rather than cultivating dispositions of other-oriented care. (Chouliaraki 2012, 180)

Chouliaraki provides a penetrating critique of the effect of neoliberal capitalism on the communicative culture of global citizen engagement. Excerpting the phrases above that begin with "rather than," the reader learns that ideal engagement must be based in selfless self-reflection on the political circumstances that contribute to suffering, which presumably would generate better responses. But, neoliberalism influences the mediated channels of advocacy, transforming engagement into an ironic performance of self-fulfillment. The ethos of Chouliaraki's approach is very much in line with the one pursued in this book, but she stops short of the deeper critique of capitalism itself and fails to explain how exactly it works to impact citizen engagement, leaving the reader shrugging.

Critical Theory of the Frankfurt School offers specific insight into why politics drops out, how culture is affected, and why solidarity is rendered impotent. But Chouliaraki opts out of the long journey, deciding instead that the Frankfurt School proposes only a "pessimistic narrative that leaves little or no ground for the promise of cosmopolitan solidarity" (2012, 29). The notion of Critical Theory as pessimistic is rooted, ostensibly, in the dead end of Horkheimer and Adorno's *The Dialectic of Enlightenment* (2002). In fact, other Frankfurt School scholars, most conspicuously Herbert Marcuse, do not share this sensibility. Even Horkheimer and Adorno have been "reclaimed" as successors have sought to rescue Critical Theory from the abyss by reconnecting the tradition to Enlightenment liberalism (Bronner 2004). Persuasively, the Frankfurt School is argued to be an heir to liberalism and Marxism, carrying the torch of emancipatory internationalism. Both in their lives and in their philosophies, contributors to the Frankfurt School embodied cosmopolitan solidarity, which makes Chouliaraki's dismissal of the whole program that much more unusual.

Rather, having "refrained from adopting the pessimistic argument of the critical school" Chouliaraki concludes that "global capitalism should not be seen as an adversary of cosmopolitan solidarity but as its necessary yet fragile condition of possibility" (2012, 204). Despite two hundred pages of materialist critique, global capitalism, presumably in its current form, remains apparently indispensable to any hope for internationalism. Again, an unusual conclusion that makes it seem like all the talk of neoliberalism was for nothing. The author suggests we focus instead on the need to "better understand and critically evaluate how the market, politics and technology come together to transform the moral dispositions of our public life—how they turn solidarity from a collectivist politics of conviction into a lifestyle politics of reflexivity" (Chouliaraki 2012, 204). And when we do this, then what? Teaching media literacy without a political program is insufficient for addressing the structural challenges to cosmopolitan political engagement. With nowhere to go and nothing to do, it's Chouliaraki that leaves us clinging only to our despair.

Critiques that evade assuming an ideological position yet traffic in the cachet and currency of Marxism are engaging in a form of troubling appropriation. Materialism Lite undercuts the value and promise of Marxist praxis by coopting the radical sentimentality of clichés about neoliberalism while rejecting the full scope and weight of its critique. Placing the "Inc." after "human rights" or calling it an "industry" or part of an "industrial complex" becomes a tired trope on the Left that begins to mean nothing very quickly. Because of the emptiness of Materialism Lite, recommitting to the analytical force of the Frankfurt School is essential.

Toward a Critical Theory of Human Rights Practice

Coherent application of Critical Theory provides a compelling theoretical framework for approaching the questions posed above. Table 2.1 articulates the outline of the book and traces how shifts in consumer capitalism fatally injure the potential for human rights advocacy to emerge as a powerful protector of human dignity. While each of the questions in the previous section is addressed throughout the text, each chapter evidences a particular theme with specific clarity (hopefully).

Chapter 3 details how an advocacy formula crystallized during the 1980s, made possible by the rise of the financial services industry, which relied on benefit concerts featuring celebrities and musicians to elicit interest in global campaigns. While entertaining the audience and making it easier for them to engage, the means of engagement inherently restrict the depth of commitment. Chapter 4 explains how the expansion of information and communications technology permits the television viewer to participate in the spectacle of the suffering other, yet only generates solidarity as gesture, with limited political value. Chapter 5 suggests that corporate marketing culture shapes human rights as simply another component of a branded lifestyle, even at the expense of core principles like truth and accuracy in reporting. Chapter 6 contains a postmortem report and current status update, as well as a vision for reclaiming human rights as a politics of resistance.

Table 2.1 A Critical Theory of human rights

	Shifts in consumer capitalism	*Posits human rights as*	*Manifests advocacy as*	*Affects crucial variable*
Chapter 3	Personal finance	Convenience	Entertainment	~Commitment
Chapter 4	Communications technology	Spectacle	Gesture	~Solidarity
Chapter 5	Corporate consolidation	Brand	Lifestyle	~Truth

Foundationally, I draw inspiration from the Critical Theory of the Frankfurt School, its scholars-in-exile, and the intellectual tradition tied to the Institute for Social Research. The Frankfurt School situates itself as heir to Hegelian Idealism interpreted through the Marxian Materialist turn. Their profound contribution to this legacy is the core notion that the repressive nature of capitalism retains its essence even as the contours of capitalism evolve. From Fordist to Taylorist modes of mass production and into the age of globalized corporate capitalism, as market forces penetrate more deeply, they continue to constitute the structure of contemporary social and cultural life. Twentieth-century Critical Theory hinges on the principle that capitalism does not only control an individual's interaction with the market in her capacity as a worker; that is, the individual's circumscribed ability to be naturally free by virtue of her alienation from the means of production. *Consumer capitalism* also colonizes leisure time and impacts personal tastes, while influencing the needs and desires that subsequently drive decisions for the individual as worker. As a dominant ideology, free market capitalism obstructs human freedom by normalizing consumerism for its own sake, compelling individuals to work more, borrow more, and, in the process, one's self grows apart from one's self-actualization. The habits conditioned by consumer capitalism bear an inverse relationship to the ability to live by the dictates of reason and in accord with human potentialities.

Critical Theory insists that consumer capitalism impedes creativity, collectivity, and common sense by injecting the psyche with values that serve the interests of capital rather than the human needs of fulfillment and emancipation. Consumerism produces self-seeking individuals that see status in the lifestyles of the owners of capital and aspire to take a seat next to their supervisors, even though class stratification remains rigidly resistant. Consumers become socialized to ignore the areas of life that constrain their human capabilities, and to privilege possessions and the significance that capitalism imparts to them. This process discredits alternative attitudes and marginalizes radical voices by relegating political perspectives that threaten the status quo. To inoculate consumers, these forces distract from the structures and systems out of which unfreedom arise by infecting culture with pacifying tendencies. Rather than permitting contradictions to disrupt daily life and prompt curiosity, consumerism provides a "totally managed world" that discourages engagement altogether (Horkheimer 2002, ix). In a society in which all goods, services, and earthly pleasures are conveniently accessible in the marketplace, individuals withdraw, dulling the impulse for public involvement and social change.

What we would call neoliberalism or market fundamentalism in contemporary terms, mid-century Critical Theorists recognized as a post-industrial capitalism that privileges the pursuit of individual self-sufficiency and demonizes empathy, solidarity, and communalism. Expressions of genuine individuality, notably in art, music, and philosophy, are replaced with homogenized products that stand in for that which used to be creatively determined. For instance, Theodor Adorno highlights the impact on jazz (1989b) and poetry (1989a), Siegfried Kracauer provides a penetrating critique of dance and film (1995), and Walter Benjamin focuses on photography (1968). The society of mass consumption values group existence only to the extent it breeds conformity and reinforces entrenched authority. Collective political action, such as worker's struggles and other social movements, is intolerable because it consists of conscious individuals seeking universal ends and threatening particularistic gain. Consumer capitalism cultivates individuals as objects instead of as subjects striving after self-determination. From this perspective, "all attempts to use the subject, construed in this sense, as the basis for constructing an intersubjective world have a dubious character" (Marcuse 1989, 62). Therefore, group cohesion manifests itself as mass hysteria, solidarity as self-indulgence, cosmopolitan internationalism as confined provincialism.

Finally, Jürgen Habermas's contribution to the Frankfurt School addresses the impact of late-capitalism on communication, which has particular resonance for this book. Through this reading, the market infects mass media and commercializes the processes and platforms through which information is shared. The quality of public debate diminishes, news morphs into commodity, and content becomes monochromatic and repetitive. "It was not merely standardization as such that established an inverse relationship between the commercialization of culture goods and their complexity, but that special preparation of products that made them consumption-ready" (Habermas 1991, 166). Public relations and advertising prefigure and manage public opinion, reducing social friction and dissent (Habermas 1991, 193–94). Through the maintenance of popular opinion, dominant narratives and hegemonic ideals are proposed and normalized. Habermas's philosophy permits the Frankfurt School to go beyond the cultural diffusion and social learning arguments that Marcuse relies on and point to particular technologies and forums through which the values of the ruling classes are transmitted. But the subject matter remains central: "the integration culture concocted and propagated by the mass media, although unpolitical in its intention, itself represents a political ideology; a political program, or any staged announcement whatsoever, must indeed not enter into competition with it but must strive for concordance" (Habermas 1991, 215). A manufactured media environment resists and marginalizes messages that challenge its supremacy or offer alternatives.

Indeed, Critical Theory possesses the analytic vigor to explain paradoxes of twenty-first-century global political life. What Herbert Marcuse calls "rational irrationality" captures the tensions of consumer capitalist society, wherein conflicting logics rest comfortably at ease with one another without provoking awareness as to their utter absurdity. Rational irrationality describes the incongruent circumstances that defy comprehension yet evade inquiry. Critical Theory compels examination that transcends contradiction, while focusing attention on the damaging impact of capitalism on radical political struggle. Political theory, to be meaningful and relevant, must be normative in nature and take human freedom as its object or risk contributing to the perpetuation of human bondage. For, as it is said, "theory is always for someone and for some purpose" (Cox 1981). If theory fails to pursue an objective, or *telos*, in line with emancipatory values, then it succeeds in providing cover for abusers and violators, whether it intends to or not. Claims to objectivity ought to be met with skepticism as symptoms of ethical detachment or pragmatic dissonance. Being honest and forthcoming about one's normative convictions is an obligation of scholars who wade into the waters of politics.

I employ Critical Theory to investigate transnational human rights advocacy because I believe the human rights movement has the potential to be a force for the preservation of human dignity but lacks the capacity for self-reflection that could legitimately improve human rights praxis. Human rights norms emerge from social movement struggles that challenge the status quo, unseat oppressive regimes, and demand institutional change. Politicized by the experience of subordination, activists embrace the radical dimensions of their cause and insist on recognition. The claim that disenfranchised groups possess dignity, deserve recognition, and must be at the center of public policy decisions contains the radical essence of human rights for the way in which it seeks to upend realpolitik. Yet with the ascent of human rights from the margins to the mainstream of global ethical discourse, and driven by the professionalized advocacy sector, the subversive qualities of human rights have been lost. Indigenous activist movements retain it certainly, but in the translation of human rights ideals to the mass audience, through advocacy NGOs that work on behalf of others, the radical political elements of human rights recede and vanish. What is left is a movement that avoids political questions and seeks the most palatable and least radical position possible. I contend that the use of consumer culture mechanisms in human rights campaigns strips away the radicalism at the heart of human rights in exchange for mass appeal. Critical Theory provides an intellectual framework to address this core dilemma by underscoring the relationship between commercialism, politics, and power.

Ultimately, a critical theory of human rights practice informs the constitutive elements of the movement and advises on the capacity for actors to make transformative change. To the extent consumerism and popular culture serve as the infrastructure for the promotion of a grassroots constituency, the social relations of human rights advocacy rest on faulty foundations. Building a mass movement should not involve building a movement of masses, but that is the shape of human rights today. Instead of aggregating quantities of individuals, gathering masses entails acquiescence to centralized authority and diffuse conformity throughout the group. The accumulation of human rights disciples conditions followers to follow and arranges the community hierarchically with the nongovernmental organization as nucleus perched atop a pedestal. Rather than unleashing the creative expression of individuality in the service of human dignity, this construction stifles innovative thinking, recycles problem solving, and routinizes crisis response. Standardizing the practice of human rights advocacy silences uniquely radical approaches to politics and circumscribes the positive consequences of these potentially important interventions.

We should not expect the human rights community to transform into a global solidarity movement, and it is a mistake to hold it up to mythic standards. However, it is reasonable to hope that transnational NGOs are capable of rethinking their position: detached from the grassroots, slow to evolve, resistant to change, politically evasive, and culturally dull. Rather than relying on cheap tactics, the human rights community must invigorate the global public by inspiring and politicizing ordinary individuals to stand up. Sustained commitment of a permanent constituency for human rights protection is possible. Sparking consciousness for the imperative to contribute to a brigade of dignity defenders is essential if human rights are to experience resurgence. The future of human rights depends upon forging relationships in which the dignity of the other—and the work required to secure that dignity—is inextricably bound with the dignity of the self. Mass appeals prevent a new utopia from taking shape. Transcending mass appeals demands cultivating global citizens with mutual obligations for the welfare of others, not consumers serving only themselves.

Note

1. For instance, see the contributions in this collection that address debates about human rights, global poverty, and neoliberalism (Lettinga and van Troost 2015).

References

Adorno, Theodor. 1989a. "Lyric Poetry and Society." In *Critical Theory and Society: A Reader*, edited by Stephen Eric Bronner and Douglas Kellner. New York: Routledge.

———. 1989b. "Perennial Fashion—Jazz." In *Critical Theory and Society: A Reader*, edited by Stephen Eric Bronner and Douglas Kellner. New York: Routledge.

Benjamin, Walter. 1968. "The Work of Art in the Age of Mechanical Reproduction." In *Illuminations: Essays and Reflections*, edited by Hannah Arendt. New York: Harcourt Brace Jovanovich.

Bob, Clifford. 2002. "Merchants of Morality." *Foreign Policy*, March 1. http://www.foreignpolicy.com/articles/2002/03/01/merchants_of_morality.

Bronner, Stephen Eric. 2004. *Reclaiming the Enlightenment: Toward a Politics of Radical Engagement*. New York: Columbia University Press.

Brown, Wendy. 2004. ""The Most We Can Hope For…": Human Rights and the Politics of Fatalism." *The South Atlantic Quarterly* 103 (2): 451–63.

Carla Winston. 2017. "Nonprofit Product Placement: Human Rights Advocacy in Film and Television." *Atlantic Journal of Communication* 25 (1): 17–32.

Chouliaraki, Lilie. 2012. *The Ironic Spectator*. Cambridge: Polity.

Cmiel, Kenneth. 1999. "The Emergence of Human Rights Politics in the United States." *The Journal of American History* 86 (3): 1231–50.

Conroy, Meredith, Jessica T. Feezell, and Mario Guerrero. 2012. "Facebook and Political Engagement: A Study of Online Political Group Membership and Offline Political Engagement." *Computers in Human Behavior* 28 (5): 1535–46. https://doi.org/10.1016/j.chb.2012.03.012.

Cox, Robert W. 1981. "Social Forces, States and World Orders: Beyond International Relations Theory." *Millennium—Journal of International Studies*, no. 10: 126–55.

Cress, Daniel M. 1997. "Nonprofit Incorporation among Movements of the Poor." *The Sociological Quarterly* 38 (2): 343–60.

De Waal, Alex. 2015. "Rethinking Activism: Social Movements and the State over the Longue Dureé." In *The Social Practice of Human Rights*. New York, NY: Palgrave Macmillan.

Delaney, Eamon. 2015. "The 'Human Rights' Industry Has Lost All Sense of Proportion." Independent.Ie, June 16. http://www.independent.ie/opinion/comment/the-human-rights-industry-has-lost-all-sense-of-proportion-31304648.html.

Eckel, Jan, and Samuel Moyn (eds.). 2013. *The Breakthrough: Human Rights in the 1970s*. Philadelphia: University of Pennsylvania Press.

Falk, Richard A. 2009. *Achieving Human Rights*. New York: Routledge.

Fawzy, Farida. 2016. "Ice Bucket Challenge Leads to Gene Discovery." CNN, July 27. http://www.cnn.com/2016/07/27/health/als-ice-bucket-challenge-funds-breakthrough/index.html.

Gladwell, Malcolm. 2010. "Small Change." *The New Yorker*, October 4. http://www.newyorker.com/reporting/2010/10/04/101004fa_fact_gladwell.

Granovetter, Mark. 1973. "The Strength of Weak Ties." *American Journal of Sociology* 78 (6): 1360–80.

Habermas, Jürgen. 1991. *The Structural Transformation of the Public Sphere: An Inquiry into a Category of Bourgeois Society*. Sixth printing edition. Cambridge, MA: The MIT Press.

Hassan, Budour. 2015. "How the Human Rights Industry Undermines Palestinian Liberation." TeleSur, December 10. http://www.telesurtv.net/english/opinion/How-the-Human-Rights-Industry-Undermines-Palestinian-Liberation-20151210-0007.html.

Henningsen, Patrick. 2016. "Smart Power and 'The Human Rights Industrial Complex'." Global Research, March 15. http://www.globalresearch.ca/smart-power-and-the-human-rights-industrial-complex/5514739.

Hopgood, Stephen. 2006. *Keepers of the Flame: Understanding Amnesty International*. Ithaca, NY: Cornell University Press.

———. 2013. *The Endtimes of Human Rights*. Ithaca, NY: Cornell University Press.

Horkheimer, Max. 2002. *Critical Theory: Selected Essays*. New York: Continuum Publishers.

Horkheimer, Max, and Theodor W. Adorno. 2002. *Dialectic of Enlightenment: Philosophical Fragments*. Cultural Memory in the Present. Stanford, CA: Stanford University Press.

INCITE! Women of Color Against Violence (ed.). 2009. *The Revolution Will Not Be Funded: Beyond the Non-profit Industrial Complex*. Unknown edition. Cambridge, MA: South End Press.

Keck, Margaret E., and Kathryn A. Sikkink. 1998. *Activists beyond Borders: Advocacy Networks in International Politics*. Ithaca: Cornell University Press.

King, Samantha. 2006. *Pink Ribbons, Inc.: Breast Cancer and the Politics of Philanthropy*, 1st ed. Minneapolis: University of Minnesota Press.

Kovalik, Daniel. 2012. "Amnesty International and the Human Rights Industry." November 8. www.counterpunch.org. http://www.counterpunch.org/2012/11/08/amnesty-international-and-the-human-rights-industry/.

Kracauer, Siegfried. 1995. *Mass Ornament: Weimar Essays*. Translated by Thomas Y. Levin. [S.l.]: Harvard University Press.

Lettinga, Doutje, and Lars van Troost (eds.). 2015. *Can Human Rights Bring Social Justice?* Strategic Studies. Amnesty International Netherlands. https://www.amnesty.nl/sites/default/files/public/can_human_rights_bring_social_justice.pdf.

Marcuse, Herbert. 1989. "Philosophy and Critical Theory." In *Critical Theory and Society: A Reader*, edited by Stephen Eric Bronner and Douglas Kellner. New York: Routledge.

McCarthy, John D., and Mayer N. Zald. 1977. "Resource Mobilization and Social Movements: A Partial Theory." *The American Journal of Sociology* 82 (6): 1212–41.

Minkoff, Debra C. 1999. "Bending with the Wind: Strategic Change and Adaptation by Women's and Racial Minority Organizations." *American Journal of Sociology* 104 (6): 1666–703.

Moyn, Samuel. 2010. *The Last Utopia: Human Rights in History*. Belknap Press of Harvard University Press.

Park, Chang Sup. 2013. "Does Twitter Motivate Involvement in Politics? Tweeting, Opinion Leadership, and Political Engagement." *Computers in Human Behavior* 29 (4): 1641–48. https://doi.org/10.1016/j.chb.2013.01.044.

Perugini, Nicola, and Neve Gordon. 2015. *The Human Right to Dominate*. New York, NY: Oxford University Press.

Piven, Frances Fox, and Richard A. Cloward. 1979. *Poor People's Movements: Why They Succeed, How They Fail*. Vintage. https://books.google.com/books?hl=en&lr=&id=qI9mzBuTvjUC&oi=fnd&pg=PR9&dq=piven+and+cloward+poor+people%27s+movement&ots=qSWKK-7qkv&sig=p-CLvmvSmVu_rrmup2cDTD1jmglg.

Pruce, Joel R. 2015. "The Practice Turn in Human Rights Research." In *The Social Practice of Human Rights*, edited by Joel R. Pruce. New York: Palgrave Macmillan.

Richey, Lisa Ann, and Stefano Ponte. 2011. *Brand Aid: Shopping Well to Save the World*. Minneapolis: University of Minnesota Press.

Rieff, David. 2003. *A Bed for the Night: Humanitarianism in Crisis*. New York: Simon & Schuster.

Singer, Peter. 1972. "Famine, Affluence, and Morality." *Philosophy & Public Affairs* 1 (3): 229–43.

———. 2011. *The Expanding Circle: Ethics, Evolution, and Moral Progress*. With a new afterword by the author edition. Princeton, NJ: Princeton University Press.

Stammers, Neil. 2009. *Human Rights and Social Movements*. London: Pluto Press.

CHAPTER 3

Benefit Concerts, Constituencies of Compassion, and the Culture Industry

Introduction

Cultivating a community of dignity defenders demands a creative vision. To attempt to skim the humanity from the crowd and channel it for the rights and welfare of others assumes, firstly, that such a thing is possible and, secondly, that doing so may have a positive impact. Due skepticism is in order because, inspecting the world, respect and regard for others are not abundant resources. However, with the rise of neoliberal capitalism, a hybrid humanistic order emerges that articulates acts that serve others in forms that also satisfy selfish impulses. Altruism framed not as asceticism, but as consumption. The suggestion that ethical action requires sacrifice—the Mother Theresa archetype—is eclipsed by a concept of global engagement linking commercialism to do-gooderism. This shift produces a resonant cultural framework and a model that audiences know how to experience and have come to recognize and expect.

Which is why, during the summer of 2005, when ten concerts occurred simultaneously in venues across the globe, all focused on ending the horrors of poverty and inequality, a trained generational sensibility responded. Featuring top talents across genres of popular music, the Live 8 events built on a legacy of charity and advocacy dating back twenty years. Audiences participated in the day's events and, like their parents before them, reveled in the sheer fun of these happenings and their own self-affirming role in confronting indignity.

J. R. Pruce, *The Mass Appeal of Human Rights*, Human Rights Interventions, https://doi.org/10.1007/978-3-319-92075-7_3

Five years later, when an earthquake shattered Haiti, the international community launched into action again. The Red Cross solicited for donations that could, for the first time, be transferred electronically via text message. Record amounts were raised, with proceeds awarded to several prominent relief organizations. Stars of stage and screen served as masters of ceremony during a televised and webcasted telethon, "Hope for Haiti Now: A Global Benefit for Earthquake Relief." One week later, dozens of artists gathered to record a single to further benefit these efforts, producing an updated version of the 1985 hit, "We Are the World." With the addition of a rap verse, the song mirrors the original and trades heavily in the powerful memories that audiences bring to each listening.

Perfectly routine by today's standards, the initiation of this model emerges as the convergence between multiple movements in the context of crucial substructural shifts. From the mid-1970s on, human rights ascended to occupy a privileged role in global life, as a powerful moral vernacular. Simultaneously, neoliberal economics rose from the arcane pages of academic journals to the white papers of public policy as an ideological framework determined to recalibrate the balance between state mechanisms and free markets. The forbearers of each field win Nobel Prizes in 1977: Dr. Milton Friedman in Economics and Amnesty International in Peace. Human rights and neoliberalism both prioritize individual freedoms and constitute liberal subjects (Odysseos 2010), though human rights protection requires a functional state, while neoliberalism anticipates the state's withdrawal. Despite contradictions, or perhaps because of them, human rights conforms to the new neoliberal order by cultivating advocates as individuals apart from the collective and by championing causes that refuse to adequately challenge the state. Privatization of industry and financialization of capital usher in a period of mass consumption that captures not only the markets, but also the imagination.

Mass campaigns for the dignity of others crystallize in an era defined by the cultural prominence of lifestyle materialism identified with "the yuppie." The consequence of this encounter reveals an advocacy sector dependent on commercialism for both financial stability, as well as its social foundation. The consumer market is also changed, however, having absorbed the moral imperative introduced by human rights and humanitarianism. Capitalism co-opts opposing ideologies and insists on the political impotence of the carcass that remains. By locating central components of human rights practice in the market, advocacy becomes commodified, transforming psychological experiences like empathy and outrage into numbing commercial transactions. Consumerism conditions and rewards self-seeking behavior, creating willful diversions that anesthetize and insulate individuals from critical thought. Caring about distant others becomes integrated into the consumer lifestyle as an accessory, like a belt or a hat—as something that signifies who we are but can be discarded and replaced if it goes out of style.

This interaction between form and content creates a new paradigm: Human rights protection becomes a fun and easy practice, while mass consumption is injected with a flaccid sense of global concern. Marketized devices utilized in these campaigns reflect strategy, shape substance, and affect the relationships constituted in the process—between advocate and victim, advocate and movement. Consumerism carves a path for NGOs to make campaign participation more convenient and less political. Manifestations of popular culture—entertainment, celebrity, merchandising—help NGOs elevate the profile of their organizations and issues. In the words of Sir Bob Geldof, what the world needed in the 1980s was "a populist, non-governmental constituency...a constituency of compassion" (1986, 250). The ability to rouse the consciousness of the general public and place a dire issue on the agenda is powerful and by a range of metrics—dollars raised, membership figures, or intensity of public outcry—the role played by consumer culture helped elevate the profile of human rights to the ranks of other mainstream liberal ideals, such as environmentalism or the ethical treatment of animals.

Though in the process of mainstreaming human rights, the political claims at core of the idea become subjugated. Campaign messaging and policy asks ignore root causes, preferring uncomplicated, uncontroversial explanations that resonate with the audience. NGOs conduct outreach to supporters not as political actors, but by relating to them as consumers—individuals with dispensable income and a predilection for self-indulgence, yet with a sense of social consciousness. By eschewing the political dimensions of indignity and suffering—that is, the ways in which power is exercised through systems and structures to bring about indignity and suffering—NGOs stake out a stance divorced from a critique of power.

This chapter offers an origin story for the model of commercialized advocacy that is routine by today's standards. Through a succession of mass cultural events initiated by Amnesty International originally, handed off to campaigns for famine alleviation in Ethiopia, and repurposed by the transnational movement to end Apartheid in South Africa, Western publics become oriented toward causes through their engagement with popular culture and mass consumption. Results are decidedly uneven. Amnesty International manages to retain and strengthen its identity, while humanitarian relief in Ethiopia presents a caricature that casts an infamous shadow. The Anti-Apartheid Movement provides an ideal-type example of the potential for mass mobilization, though is only possible due to a decades-long grassroots struggle. Advocacy makes gains. Aid presents a cautionary tale. Activism gets the goods. At stake at this auspicious moment is the soul and identity of the human rights community constituted through a confrontation between the political imperatives of mass movements for human dignity and the seductive features of consumer capitalism. In order to produce a robust analysis of this period and the trends in human rights advocacy, socioeconomic context provides a lens through which to understand *why* it was possible for this model to take the form it did *when* it did.

The Birth of the Society of Mass Consumption

Consumer culture first arises as an outgrowth of the affluence in the USA following World War II. Suburban sprawl and Madison Avenue dominated society and perpetuated the blurring of class lines. The integration of economic justice demands into postwar social welfare arrangements and the continued disintegration of organized labor generally resulted in marginalizing the working class. The expanding middle and upper classes projected their lifestyles downward through popular culture, influencing the preferences of the lower classes. Following Herbert Marcuse:

> Here the so-called equalization of class distinctions reveals its ideological function. If the worker and his boss enjoy the same television program and visit the same resort places, if the typist is as attractively made up as the daughter of her employer, if the Negro owns a Cadillac, if they all read the same newspaper, then this assimilation indicates not the disappearance of classes, but the extent to which the needs and satisfactions that serve the preservation of the Establishment are shared by the underlying population. (Marcuse 1964, 8)

The crucial point in this analysis is the change in the composition of society and its effect on the psychology of those getting left behind. In Gramscian terms, the “hegemony” of upper-class ideologies about consumption and the good life are personified as those values that should be held by all, despite the fact that they impede the realization of the self and human emancipation. For Marcuse, this is manifested in commodity consumption. The more one owns, the "better" one is, the freer one is. Freedom is exercised by the choices one makes in the marketplace, without regard for the relations of production. This compulsion for consumerism is a form of social control that permeates the lower classes at their own expense, and the deeper consumers buy into this mantra, the more alienated from actualization they become.

But for Marcuse, this is not simply a story about luxury automobiles and vacation resorts: Consumerism infects politics. Radical, emancipatory politics are rendered impotent when the torchbearers of progressive movements, the working class and the Left, become absorbed into the society of mass consumption. As diverse segments of society converge on the market, a collapsing effect ripples outward. Consumers are submerged in the notion that any problem can be alleviated through the purchase of goods and services, thereby making it unnecessary to *politically* challenge power structures. The misery and pain of daily life can be ignored when consumers are pacified by the newest home entertainment system or blockbuster action film. Radical challenges to the status quo are relegated, and the society of mass consumption becomes ultimately one-dimensional—that is, devoid of nonconformist perspectives. "And if the individuals are pre-conditioned so that the satisfying goods also include thoughts, feelings, aspirations, why should they wish to think, feel, and imagine for themselves?" (Marcuse 1964, 50). One-dimensionality is the collapse of multiple, contrarian perspectives in favor of a singular, flat vision for society.

Yet, the society of mass consumption was not confined to the economic and political realms. The cultural realm was invaded as well through the mechanism of the "culture industry." Theodor Adorno and Max Horkheimer are the pioneers of this area of Critical Theory for their insights into the encroachment of the forces of production into culture. For them, this advancement is the logical progression of the system of capitalism that had successfully colonized labor and now was extending its control over non-work, or leisure time. The culture industry is the expression of social control exercised over consumers in their free time. "The effectiveness of the culture industry depends not on its parading an ideology, on disguising the true nature of things, but in removing the thought that there is any alternative to the status quo" (Adorno 1991, 11). At stake is the effect of culture on critical thought, on the ability of the audience to seek self-consciousness and social awareness.

The claim, emphasized most clearly by Marcuse, entails the numbing of the general public and the stifling of radical political perspectives by cultural hegemony: "there is no reason to insist on self-determination if the administered life is the comfortable and even the 'good' life. This is the rational and material ground for the unification of opposites, for one-dimensional political behavior. On this ground, the transcending political forces *within* society are arrested, and qualitative change appears possible only as a change from *without*" (Marcuse 1964, 49). Mass cultural production masks class conflict and obscures contradictions in social life that could generate revolutionary activity. Instead, the viewer and listener are placated by feelings of satisfaction, happiness, and freedom that the consumption of popular culture falsely suggests.

Popular music, one product of the culture industry, is particularly engineered for ensuring passivity among its audience due to the standardization with which it is produced, mirroring the routinization and mechanization inherent in industrial capitalism. Adorno describes this phenomenon as an expression of the "fetish character in music" (1991, 29). Hit songs are designed for "regressive listening" that "appears as soon as advertising turns into terror, as soon as nothing is left for the consciousness but to capitulate before the superior power of the advertised stuff and purchase spiritual peace by making the imposed goods literally its own thing" (Adorno 1991, 47–48). This cultural form sells an image, an individuality, that it in reality suffocates. It is the illusion of free choice in the cultural marketplace that consumers succumb to in their search for personal expression. "[T]he official culture's pretense of individualism...necessarily increases in proportion to the liquidation of the individual...The identical character of the goods which everyone must buy hides itself behind the rigor of the universally compulsory style" (Adorno 1991, 40). Instead of fulfilling the emotional desire to seek out and experience art, popular music is force-fed to the consumer. The culture industry treats consumers like children and perpetuates regressive cultural behavior with the rhythmic structure of the songs, as well as through the production process and manner of delivery (Barber 2007). The postwar economic explosion widens class division, while dulling the impulse to fight for something better. When neoliberalism enters the fray, its advocates present an argument for institutionalizing these divisions justified by an ideology that compellingly adopts the language of freedom—but a freedom now understood in a negative sense. Rather than growing a functioning and robust social welfare state, neoliberal advocates described a freedom secured only through individual pursuits in the marketplace. The profound affluence and culture return to mass consumption in the 1980s sits in contrast against the backdrop of the economic instability of the prior decade.

The 1970s was a period of perpetual crisis and societal despair, highlighted by oil spikes, inflation, and a general transformation of the economic landscape. The Third World was industrializing and inviting foreign direct investment from the West. This trend continued when the Organization of the Petroleum Exporting Countries (OPEC) began to exert control over flows of oil and money—especially in response to flare-ups in conflict between Arab states and Israel during the decade. Western economic preponderance was slipping away, and the balance of power was shifting. Growth slowed dramatically. Recession ensued. Volatility in the energy market, coupled with the adaptations made by industrial nations to deal with floating exchange rates and a weak dollar, shaped the 1970s into a period of "anxiety, fear for the future—in short, crisis" (Beaud 2001, 232).

However, in the 1980s, US markets would tourniquet their wounds and generate positive flows by opening investment to individuals. With the deregulation of finance in 1975, the exchange of stocks moved from fixed commission rates to competitive commission rates and initiated the personalization of finance with discount brokerage firms (Nocera 1994, 106–7). "Deregulation of financial services was oriented toward creating a consumer rather than business face for stock ownership" (Martin 2002, 23). Money market funds, first devised in the late 1960s, were the vehicle for introducing middle-class consumers to the stock market as a mechanism for "saving" money; traditionally reliable dividends were perceived as interest returned on principal from a high-yield savings account. Inflation compelled this move because as the value of money fell, actual savings accounts (regulated by federal rates) fell. "A blurring had begun between saving and investing" (Nocera 1994, 83).

Because money market funds were not backed by the Federal Reserve, they were resistant to inflation. While returns were higher in the market than in savings, consumers kept their money in these funds and became accustomed to moving money back and forth according to changes in interest rates (Nocera 1994, 83). Money market managers profited by establishing these funds and charging transaction fees to users. Personal finance extended beyond the savings account, and investment was no longer exclusively for big business. What started as a mechanism for individuals to sidestep the pitfalls of inflation accounted for $400 billion in investment by 1991; this "was the first truly different wrinkle in personal finance since the credit card" and would facilitate change in "the financial habits of the middle class" (Nocera 1994, 75). Personal debt, in the form of credit cards and home mortgages, accelerated this trend throughout the decade as a reflection of the imperative for consumption that defined the 1980s.

The presumed profitability of money market funds, however, would be juxtaposed with an unprecedented accumulation of debt that "turned 'the eighties' into a term of opprobrium" (Nocera 1994, 297). Accessibility of personal lines of credit ushered in and perpetuated consumption for its own sake. By all measures, debt skyrocketed during the decade and by 1987 the upward trend peaked as total consumer debt had doubled, revolving credit card balances tripled, home equity loans amounted to $80 billion of new debt annually, and the ratio of debt payment to disposable income per household was 25% (Nocera 1994, 297). Specifically, credit cards were a central driver of this trend. "By 1984, 71 percent of all Americans between seventeen and sixty-five carried a credit card" (Nocera 1994, 301).

The blurring that had begun with money market funds had been transferred to the notion of credit and debt as a normal component of one's financial portfolio—as if the money one is allowed to borrow from a lender was real, earned money that consumers were entitled to. Personal finance in the 1980s took the form of market investment and debt, replacing the 1970s austerity mind-set. Instead, individuals consumed above their class and beyond their means, in such a way that has been characterized as "a betrayal of traditional middle-class values" and "a wholesale surrender to the priorities of profit and the pleasures of consumerism" (Ehrenreich 1989, 200).

Beyond the pleasurable benefit of purchasing material goods, consumerism is embedded with social meaning. Finance and banking during this period personified the upper crust of society because of the way in which it had emerged as the preeminent growth sector. Those employed in this area benefited quickly and directly from changes in the economy. The credit card industry had become the "most profitable activity in all of banking" (Nocera 1994, 302), and "by 1985, close to 8 million Americans…were using them to ring up close to $8 billion in charges" (Nocera 1994, 303). As finance charges and overdraft fees flooded in, lenders—the companies, their boards of trustees and shareholders—reaped enormous profits. This was true in investment as well, as tycoons rose to prominence as titans of industry.

The cultural projection of Gordon Gekko captured something unique about the era by embodying real-life figures like Donald J. Trump and T. Boone Pickens. The persona of Michael Douglas's character in the film *Wall Street* (1987) was a caricature of the age, but not a fiction. Wealth inequalities were widening and class distinctions continuing to erode. Penthouse apartments, chauffeur-driven limousine rides to work, and thousand-dollar suits constitute an idealized lifestyle. And, for some, it was a reality. "In Wall Street's bustling money factories, the goal of amassing a million by age thirty was neither uncommon nor entirely unrealistic. Baby high-rollers were proliferating, and New York's $50-a-lunch restaurants were jammed, by the late eighties, with fresh-faced young people barely above the drinking age" (Ehrenreich 1989, 212).

These "baby high-rollers" were also known colloquially by another name: yuppies. When *Newsweek* declared 1985 to be "The Year of the Yuppie," its editors were commenting (not unfavorably) on the compulsion toward mass consumption driven by these upper-class elites (Adler et al. 1984). Derived from the term "young, urban professionals," the yuppie was also related to the "yippie" or members of the Youth International Party, a radical social group from the late 1960s. There was a sense in which the 1960s, baby boomer generation had grown up and grown out of its youthful indiscretion in favor of a mature, profit-oriented outlook. Their resolve remains the same: the capacity of this generation to change the course of war, culture, and society by their own will. They are confident, optimistic, and undeterred by what seem like structural obstacles—be they racial discrimination or a traditional middle-class value system. The political constitution of the baby boomers is invoked in the rallying cries of the human rights campaigns of the period.

But, beyond this, yuppies are renowned for their consumption: of European cars, vacations, condos in a gentrified neighborhood, running shoes, gym memberships, and *crème fraiche* (Adler et al. 1984). The more exotic, the more expensive, the better. With more money than one needs, especially if a man was one half of a two-income family (a relatively recent trend), "the importance of status-motivated consumption increased significantly":

> A new kind of consumer had emerged for whom consumption itself came to play a central role in constructing new senses of identity based on and around the possession of status-conferring goods. Traditional concepts of social class based on education and occupation were breaking down...'Lifestyle' grew in importance as an indicator of social group

> membership, and these group identities, freed from the old restrictions imposed by social class and fixed status groups, were secured by adopting appropriate patterns of consumption. (Mason 1998, 130)

The affluent, comfortable classes embodied the mantra of excess in consumption that epitomized the 1980s as "Lifestyles of the Rich and Famous" became required viewing for all. "As the baby boom matured, spending on entertainment and recreation grew rapidly...With most of Americans' basic needs met, they have devoted an increasing share of their spending to having fun" (Russell 1993, 66). To be sure, yuppies were not a majority of the population and were likely only about 5% of their generation (Ehrenreich 1989, 198). However, the crucial point to emphasize is the influence and the impact that the objectification of the yuppie as the ideal has on lower classes: the contradiction of working people striving to obtain the lifestyle of the yuppies in a sluggish economic environment.

Yet, as the upper classes relished the good life of "champagne wishes and caviar dreams," the other 95% suffered under stagnating wages, high unemployment, and aggressive attacks on organized labor. Reaganomics and Thatcherism enacted tax cuts for the rich, which resulted in public spending cutbacks that disproportionately affected lower classes. Meanwhile, "the number of Americans living below the poverty line increased by 28 percent in just ten years, from 24.5 million in 1978 to 32 million in 1988" (Galbraith 1992, 107). Coupled with an outright attack on organized labor, the social order and future outlook of the working classes were disrupted. In the midst of recession, with the gap between rich and poor continuing to widen, those on the bottom looked upward for inspiration and Gordon Gekko smiled smugly right back at them.

Rising debt from home equity loans and revolving credit card balances were tools that working people utilized to attain a measure of the yuppie lifestyle, even if it was perpetually out of reach. Working extra hours, taking an additional mortgage on the house, and applying for another line of credit might secure a new home stereo system, but it would also set one further back—like struggling in a pool of quicksand. The cultural hegemony of consumerism projected by the yuppie against the reality of the working and middle classes shaped the needs and desires of those worst off. This is so much the case that, not only were the goods and services that credit cards could help one obtain a measure of status, but also the medium itself was culturally transformed.

> Credit cards were a status symbol. Credit cards were temptation incarnate. Credit cards could get you access to things that were otherwise out of reach. Credit cards could ruin your life. Credit cards could bring great joy. Credit cards could bring enormous misery. Of all the symbols of the American consumer society, credit cards had a hold on the subconscious that was matched—in a completely different way only by the automobile. (Nocera 1994, 300)

This final comment is especially appropriate, in terms of the comparison of the 1980s to the original era of mass consumption in the 1950s, when the automobile was introduced to the middle-class demographic for the first time. Mass consumption and the affluent lifestyle never went away but did suffer setbacks during the 1970s wave of economic crisis. In the 1980s, with the revolutions in personal finance underway, a broader swath of the population gets swept up in the "joys" of consumerism that cloud self-consciousness and affect all areas of society, from leisure and family life to labor and politics. Thus, the emergence of a human rights movement with mass appeal is mired in a cultural environment rampant with mass consumption, making market-based platforms for advocacy attractive on the one hand, as well as ripe for critique.

Burdens of Growth and Uncertain Futures

Amnesty International's genesis is nearing the status of fabled legend: In 1961, Peter Benenson wrote an opinion piece in the *Observer* entitled "The Forgotten Prisoners" that detailed the plight of Portuguese students who had been arrested and imprisoned for toasting to freedom. Much has been said of the organization's evolution, the expansion of its mandate, and its role as international "norm entrepreneur" (Larsen 1979; Clark 2001; Power 2001; Hopgood 2006). Amnesty has risen from its humble beginnings in a barrister's office in London, to become the face of the global human rights movement. Yet, the 1970s was a genuine moment of growth for the still-young NGO. Every year during the decade witnessed rapid growth by all indications. From 1969 to 1976, membership experienced a sixfold explosion, rising from 15,000 to 97,000, and the organization's annual budget expanded by over 1300 percent from approximately $43,000 to over $579,000.[1] This correlation describes the scale of growth and suggests why AI's central administrative body, the International Secretariat (IS), was forced to develop its research capacities to keep up pace with demand.

These pressures were magnified because the organization is structured in a simultaneously centralized and decentralized fashion: The production of profiles of the Prisoners of Conscience (POC) falls to the IS and its research wing, while letter writing and the work of getting prisoners freed are delegated to local chapters that adopt particular cases. Thus, the greater the number of chapters, the greater the demand on the IS to support them with reliable information and campaigns behind which to place their efforts. This tension must be emphasized because growth of this magnitude becomes difficult to manage.

However, the strain on resources was significant, not only due to the increasing demand on research, but also due to the global recession during these tough years. Financially, AI is also arranged through a combination of central and decentral relations. National sections are responsible for funding an overwhelming percentage of the IS budget through the direct contribution of its membership dues, while the central body is also involved in generating revenue through donations and sales of publications and merchandise. Furthermore, membership dues ranged widely based on the economic capacity of the national sections, their local chapters, and individual members themselves. Nobody was excluded from membership due to lack of payment and the levels of contribution were flexible. Therefore, when oil crises strike particularly hard or inflation rises dramatically, both of which happened throughout the 1970s, individual contributions were inconsistent. Relying heavily on small, voluntary donations proved to be an unsustainable system for maintaining a steady cash flow, which eventually compelled the organization to think creatively about fund-raising.

Trepidations about the balance between growth and capital, between the impulse toward expansion and the realities inherent in expansion, were expressed annually in the Treasurer's Report. While it is presumably the role of the financial officer to voice caution and advocate for incrementalism, the tone of each subsequent year's report communicates a genuine concern for the future viability of an organization growing at such an accelerated pace. Kevin T. White, in his Treasurer's Report of 1974, articulates this concern clearly:

> …as the need for AI's work grows, a melancholy fact that is all too evident, there will be continuous calls for the expansion of the organization.
>
> In our desire to meet every call, we should be conscious of the fact that we cannot immediately rectify all the ills of the world, that our resources

> are limited and that we may have to consider whether it is better to concentrate on doing effectively within our resources what we can do in a limited field, rather than spread our efforts too thinly over a broad front that we risk effectively accomplishing too little for too many…we may only be building up an expensive machine costing too much to service. (Amnesty International 1974a, 151)

The risk confronting the organization, of folding under its own weight, was a real one that was revisited in White's 1976 Report.

> Some of the arguments in favor of expanding present activities and taking on extra activities are seductive. But succumbing to these pressures would either result in partial suspension of the work AI was founded to perform under its statute (…), or in having to increase our budget substantially to enable us to continue our normal activities while taking on new tasks.
>
> I suggest that the time has come to consider how big do we want this organization to grow and whether substantial growth in the International Secretariat will result in greater effectiveness and achievements. In my view it is essential that we do not allow ourselves to be blindly borne along on a wave of enthusiasm without fully considering and appreciating the consequences. (Amnesty International 1976, 206)

At stake in this debate was the reputation AI had worked to establish—of its reliability and effectiveness—and the mandate and mission of the organization.

The question of mission has always been a crucial one for Amnesty, which historically framed itself with a limited purview. Originally cast as a protector of freedom of opinion and religion (and defender of "Prisoners of Conscience"), AI expanded its scope to focus on torture and the death penalty; these two particular violations grew out of country reporting in the 1970s flash points like Uruguay, Argentina, the Soviet Union, Chile, Iran, and Iraq. While these three pillars—Prisoners of Conscience, torture, and execution—are subsumed in the category of political and civil rights, even AI's conception of this category is limited. There was little or no work done in the areas of gender equity, slavery, privacy, family, children, or voting, for instance. Arbitrary arrest and detention, AI's initial cause, remained central to the organization's work, yet lesser violations of due process were not given much attention.

This circumscribed scope is not an accident, but a purposeful strategy. The institution itself was aware of its limitations, as Thomas Hammarberg, Chairman of the International Executive Committee in 1978, reflects: "We do not cover a broader spectrum [of rights]. This is not because we ignore the importance of all the other rights, but because we recognize that we can only achieve concrete results within set limits" (Amnesty International 1978, 1). Self-consciousness of this nature provides an intimate glimpse into the internal debate, as decision makers within the organization weigh the opportunity and challenge of growth and expansion. With this in mind, the architects of Amnesty International during the 1970s slowly created space, within the framework of the mandate, to build on areas of strength and, in a controlled fashion, raise its profile through the production of influential work.

In 1972, Amnesty International launched its Campaign Against Torture, which required raising the annual budget projections without knowing well where the money would come from to support the development of the initial torture report and the subsequent work in maintaining the campaign (Amnesty International 1973a). The initial push culminated in a December 1973 international conference in Paris, featuring a full-length film, *The Year of the Torturer*, and performances by Joan Baez (Amnesty International 1973b). Also in 1973, the International Executive Committee voted to take on the worldwide abolition of the death penalty as an addition to AI's platform (Thompson 2008).

Finally, this stance positioned AI to take on the issue of "extrajudicial executions," or summary political killings of infamy from places like Uganda, Cambodia, and Iraq, and perpetrated by "death squads" notoriously operating throughout Latin America during this period (Clark 2001, Chapter 5). In these areas and others, Amnesty began producing targeted reports on specific countries and was recognized for its groundbreaking work on Argentina's Dirty War with the 1977 Nobel Peace Prize. With these developments, Amnesty International significantly broadened its scope and burdened itself with an even larger workload during times of increasingly tighter budgetary constraints.

There is a spiraling nature to Amnesty's work: The more its research capacity improves and the more effectively it exposes violations to the world, the more work it creates for itself. As Amnesty spread out geographically, opening its first chapter behind the Iron Curtain in Moscow in 1974 (Larsen 1979, 86), new members solicited for more prisoners to represent. While the growth of national sections plateaued by the late

1970s, local groups continued to mushroom at nearly the same pace, placing additional expectations on the IS for research and case adoption. Due to these rudimentary organizational questions concerning finances and objectives, Amnesty was compelled to dig deeper and seek out new ways to fund its growing enterprise. Responding to the pressure of these developments, a strategy emerged for attracting people to the cause of human rights, building a membership base, and raising significant amounts of money for the movement.

Emergence of the Human Rights Benefit Concert

Financing the Amnesty International movement has always been a delicate matter because of the rigidly principled doctrine that governs fund-raising. In order to maintain independence, which is seen as the cornerstone of its persona, AI refuses to take government money and only rarely accepts foundation donations. Forsaking this commitment would amount to surrendering its ability to assert the universal perspective in defense of human dignity, a stance that hinges on its non-ideological and unbiased grounding. Amnesty International relies on the position it has carefully staked out for itself: a reasonable, trustworthy voice of moral authority, untainted by the corruption of self-interest. During the hyper-ideological years of the late 1970s, criticisms of AI came from both the right and the left, from democratic and communist governments, from theocracies and military dictatorships.

In this environment arose the question of *how* and *where* to raise the funds necessary to maintain, as well as expand, Amnesty's capacities. The International Secretariat tasked national sections and local groups to begin generating additional funds with renewed urgency. In the newsletters that served as the main method for communication and dissemination of directives, the IS solicited for fund-raising ideas to be submitted and reprinted in the monthly installments. "Sections and groups are invited to submit successful techniques they have used for raising funds for AI…Group 2 of Pinneberg, West Germany, for example raised 1,300 marks (about $250) during the 1972 Prisoner of Conscience Week by the simple device of preparing a huge cauldron of hot pea soup and dispensing it to passers-by on a cold Saturday morning" (Amnesty International 1974b). Two months later, it was announced that "Group 4 of the Norwegian Section raised 20,000 Norwegian kroner last November in a one-day sale of antiques, paintings, sculpture, books, and other works of art. Group Number 2 of the Danish Section raised 900 Danish kroner with an evening of folk dancing which was combined with a fashion show at which sandwiches, coffee and second-hand clothes were sold" (Amnesty International 1974c). Local efforts designed to help resolve the budget crisis took shape as cultural gatherings where supporters of AI could donate small amounts and contribute to a larger cause in the aggregate. In 1976, the UK section treads a similar path, but on a grander scale, using its own national cultural resources, setting into motion a trend that would define the period.

At this point, Amnesty International's coffers were essentially empty and the organization teetered on the edge of bankruptcy, while facing enormous pressures to produce (Biskind 2004, 44; Harrington 1986). Peter Luff, then-Assistant Director of Amnesty International, received a check at the AI-UK office from an individual donor signed "J. Cleese" (Scheinman 2008). The check was from John Cleese of Monty Python's Flying Circus, and Luff considered whether Cleese might want to be involved in fund-raising in a more central capacity. The proposal to host an event featuring high-profile comedians centered around Cleese, and presented the opportunity to raise the exposure of Amnesty International itself, a general awareness for human rights issues, as well as much needed funds. Cleese, collaborating with music and television producer, Martin Lewis, founded the events known as the Secret Policeman's Ball. "A Poke in the Eye (with a Sharp Stick)," as the first official show was called, was held in 1976 at Her Majesty's Theater and raised $40,000 for Amnesty by bringing together Cleese and his comedic comrades (McCall 1991, 46; Harrington 1986).

The first three events are considered landmark events in the history of British comedy because of the fact that they assembled two legendary comedy troupes, Beyond the Fringe and Monty Python, on one stage for the first time ever. Beyond the Fringe was of a previous generation and known for its erudite commentary and literate characters. Python was a younger crew, popular among a wider audience, for its mix of slapstick, non-sequitur, and satire. The third annual show broadened the entertainment program to include composer John Williams and guitarist Pete Townshend of The Who. As the years went on, the shows grew in prominence, were better attended, and more lucrative. In 1981, its profile was raised once again by the inclusion of hugely popular musicians like Sting, Eric Clapton, Phil Collins, and Bob Geldof. Performers, drawn to the event by its humanitarian impetus, donated their services for no compensation. The Secret Policeman's Ball was the singular, mostly directly influential ingredient for the mass benefit concerts to follow, including Geldof's Live Aid.

The live Amnesty events were recorded and sold as record albums and movies. Harvey and Bob Weinstein, at the time unproven American film producers who would go on to found Miramax Pictures and are considered highly influential figures (the former now a disgraced sexual predator), distributed *The Secret Policeman's Ball* for the American audience. Screening the film at a popular Los Angeles festival in 1982 catapulted the series to higher levels and went on to generate $6 million in revenue (Biskind 2004, 46). It is unclear precisely how much of that Amnesty International ever saw, but, as Martin Lewis has said, "What they'd [the Weinsteins] said to us was that the theatrical [release] was going to generate more publicity and heat for the home video and TV. Was Amnesty unhappy? Our expectations on this were minimal, zero. Amnesty was thrilled beyond words" (quoted in Biskind 2004, 46). The franchise spun off comedy and music albums and in-theater and at-home versions of the stage show. Having surpassed their modest goals, these benefit events went on hiatus until their re-emergence in 1987.

During these years, the USA section of AI fed off the success of the American exposure to the Secret Policeman's Ball events and sought to capitalize on the public fervor around humanitarian issues. In 1984, following a large donation by rock band U2 generated from the proceeds of a December 3 show at Radio City Music Hall in New York City, AIUSA Executive Director Jack Healey began pursuing the young Irish rock band to headline a future concert tour to celebrate Amnesty's twenty-fifth birthday (McGee 2006). By August 1985, Healey had a commitment from U2 to headline a tour set to stop in six American cities, named "The Conspiracy of Hope Tour," and would feature a reunited Police, Peter Gabriel, Jackson Browne, Lou Reed, and Joan Baez (a veritable encore of her 1973 performances in Paris), among others. For Bono of U2 and Sting of The Police, the root of their affiliation with Amnesty was their association with the Secret Policeman's Ball, Bono as a viewer, Sting as a performer (Fricke 1986, 99). The purpose of the tour was to enlist 25,000 new American members committed to write one letter a month for one year toward the release of six Prisoners of Conscience adopted for the tour: Lee Kwang-Ung (South Korea); Hugo de Leon Palacios (Guatemala); Tatyana Semyonova Osipova (USSR); Riad al-Turk (Syria); Thozamile Gqweta (South Africa); and Nguyen

Chi Thien (Vietnam) (Morley 1986, 56). By the end of this first event, AIUSA had matched its annual budget in revenue ($3 million raised), tripled its membership (45,000 newly enlisted), and secured the release of four of the six POCs (McGee 2006).

Following the enormous success of Conspiracy of Hope, Healey set his sights higher, hoping to broaden the scope of the project, while adapting the project's goals. Instead of quantitative thresholds, Healey shifted his language toward a more abstract agenda: "This was always planned as a consciousness-raising event, not a fund-raising one" (Henke 1988b, 15). Therefore, the 1988 "Human Rights Now!" tour, coinciding with the fortieth anniversary of the Universal Declaration, set out to visit and perform in countries throughout the world over a six-week period, from London, Paris, and Budapest to India, Zimbabwe, and Brazil. Playing to hundreds of thousands of people, the tour aimed at promoting the UDHR primarily and Amnesty secondarily. However, a project of this scale would be an overwhelming undertaking even for the ambitious Healey, and shortly after development had begun, it became clear that the financial cost of the tour was unsustainable.

Therefore, AI sought a partnership to help underwrite the tour and settled on Reebok, a producer of athletic apparel who agreed to fund 50% of the total cost ($8 million) and front overhead as well ($2 million); the other approximately $9 million would be recouped by ticket prices, merchandising, and the sale of broadcast rights (Henke 1988b, 15). Given AI's financial rigidity, forging a private-sector partnership was a new horizon. Yet, Healey himself oversaw the negotiations and performed a comprehensive background check of all of Reebok's operations. What he found allayed all concerns, as Reebok had already pulled out of Apartheid South Africa and subsequently established the Reebok Human Rights Award, an annual prize still in existence (Henke 1988a, 17). It is estimated that 1.2 million people worldwide attended the concerts and witnessed performances by Sting, Peter Gabriel, Tracy Chapman, Bruce Springsteen and the E Street Band, the Senegalese star Youssou N'Dour, as well as local featured artists (Rolling Stone 1988, 118). Without question, the Amnesty International profile had never been grander. The human rights movement had run away with the concept of the benefit concert. Despite its ambitions being considerably larger than its budget could withstand, Amnesty's ability to internationalize the benefit concert, coupled with the request for membership dues and the demand for political action, proved to be an effective formula for the accomplishment of its objectives.

The problems faced by AI during its early period were good problems to have: How do we carefully grow our organization in the face of vociferous calls for greater capacity? Confronted with this dilemma, its engineers made a reasonable attempt to raise money and awareness for Amnesty's operations through the use of local celebrities soliciting for donations from the public. The final analysis of this period in AI's history is definitive: These methods bolstered the budget, fostered immense growth of membership numbers, and transformed Amnesty into a global actor. By the early 1980s, international membership figures surpassed the half million mark and the IS budget approached $2 million. Over the course of a decade, these numbers climbed in lockstep by approximately ten times.

Audiences of newcomers formed first associations with human rights participation through their attendance at benefit concerts, as well as through the purchase of merchandise. But, in the case of Amnesty International, the economic act does not constitute the whole of the relationship. Because AI consists of members, dues are not simply a gift to the organization, but a symbol of commitment to the cause. Membership, even when entered into for a small fee, signals concern for the cause and the desire to contribute support—a modest commitment and a minimal personal sacrifice, but one that is socially and politically significant.

In addition to the contribution of membership dues, Amnesty has always emphasized the dimension of action. Letter writing has been the core of AI's platform from its inception. While one need not be a dues-paying member to write a letter, the format of regular member meetings at which people gather to focus on casework is the cornerstone of the movement: local chapters of ordinary people working on behalf of a prisoner or broader issue. In important ways, the membership model is that which is most familiar in the context of a local organization, not a global one. Passing around the basket at the end of a meeting is a reasonable and limited way for a community group to raise money. Membership dues are a simple way to invest activists in the organization, as well as generate funds for central operating expenses. The possibility of building a permanent, standing human rights movement was paramount in the minds of the architects, and the membership model was their way of articulating the necessity for investment and commitment. It was not sufficient for the members to serve as donors, and the letter-writing campaigns evidence the participatory nature of Amnesty International.

On balance, the integration of human rights advocacy with popular culture opened up space for meaningful public engagement. Anchored in Amnesty's signature style, humble and disciplined, commodification could be restrained. Celebrities were utilized for a purpose, foregrounding the content and the purpose. Political prisoners remained the focus, not merely featured as props. However, the risks inherent in commercialized crisis response would be laid bare when, untethered by the political orientation of human rights advocacy, humanitarian aid appeals become subjected to market forces of commodification.

Mass Events, Famine Relief, and Rock "n" Roll

The Amnesty International benefit events that began on a small scale expanded quickly from theaters and concert halls to arenas and stadiums; even wider audiences were reached through the secondary marketing and sales of films and albums. This transition, from intimate shows to mass events, is a crucial transformation in the history of "charity rock" and is largely attributed to one person: Sir Bob Geldof. Before the Secret Policeman's Ball, George Harrison's Concert for Bangladesh in 1971 was the one predecessor to set the tone for the larger concerts of the 1980s, as a singular event staged to generate funds for disaster relief in southern Asia. With this model in mind and inspired by his personal involvement with Amnesty, Bob Geldof set off on his own humanitarian expedition inspired by a *BBC* report by Michael Buerk on October 23, 1984, which described a "biblical famine" underway in war-torn Ethiopia.

In now-infamous imagery, a young British nurse was surrounded by upward of 85,000 starving people, clamoring for rations (Elliot 2005). The BBC report was not the first time the audience came face-to-face with the Ethiopian famine. "After a Save the Children Fund report on hunger in northern Ethiopia in early 1983, a television appeal in Britain raised almost £2 million. In July 1984, more than three months before the Buerk reports, ITV had shown a full-length documentary *Seeds of Despair* shot over many weeks as famine tightened its group. Another public appeal was then launched which raised almost £10 million" (Gill 2012, 37). Yet, when Geldof saw this particular spot on television, he was motivated to do something grandiose to bring relief to those Ethiopians suffering from easily remediable circumstances and began to assemble the organization that would become known as Band Aid and the concert, Live Aid.

Band Aid and Live Aid rivaled in spectacle the news report that spawned their existence. In December 1984, Band Aid, composed of UK rockers Phil Collins, George Michael, David Bowie, Boy George, Queen, U2, Duran Duran, and others, released the perennial holiday hit "Do They Know Its Christmas?" A lamentation on inequality, the song launched during the holidays in UK and USA and played on seasonal themes of concern and generosity familiar to the mainstream audience. The lyrics contrast the spirit of giving, of warmth, and of happiness that accompanies the Christmas season in the West to the negligence and desperation of "Africa." "As Ethiopians have pointed out ever since, they did of course know it was Christmas because the starving were mainly Christians" (Gill 2012, 12). Furthermore, in the dawning era of Music Television (MTV), the music video captures the arrival of the artists at the studio and the recording of the single. As will be detailed in the next chapter, graphic imagery of famine in news media and photojournalism has a long legacy dating back to the Congo in 1960. Yet, in the music video for this monumental song, there is no imagery of famine—only a behind-the-scenes look at pop stars rehearsing and carousing with one another. This visual presentation suggests an intentional detachment of the donor audience from the aid recipients, facilitated through popular culture; this alienated linkage focused attention on the celebrities as conduits of the humanitarian message but maintains the audience at a safe emotional distance from the victims' suffering.

Simultaneously, Geldof was in preparation for Live Aid, a massive concert to be held six months later in three international cities, Philadelphia, London, and Sydney (Ullestad 1992, 41) that also boasted satellite concerts in Moscow, Cologne, Yugoslavia, the Hague, Holland, Vienna, and Norway (Hillmore 1985). The events were broadcast to a worldwide audience of between 1.5 and 2 billion people, with syndicated telethons in twenty-two countries that asked viewers to give of themselves to assist those less fortunate (Coleman 1990). Despite modest projections, the initial take from these mega-events reached \$67 million (Garofalo 1992b, 27) and the subsequent sale of books and miscellaneous merchandise eventually topped \$120 million (Ockenfels and Tannenbaum 1990). This money was earmarked for specific development projects, such as "the purchase of water-drilling rigs to help with irrigation; various agricultural projects, including reforestation; medical aid; and the purchase of trucks and trailers for transportation of food and supplies" (quoted in Garofalo 1992b, 28).

Despite the panoply of critiques against which Live Aid is vulnerable (some of which will be explored below), there was a deliberate decision to frame the purpose around emergency aid for suffering people. "Long-term aid is less exciting than the Seventh Calvary arriving with food to bring people back to life," admits Geldof (quoted in Garofalo 1992b, 28). Live Aid became a seminal moment in the history of popular culture and politics because of the wave of copycat events it inspired: Farm Aid, Fashion Aid, Sports Aid, Hear'n Aid, Visual Aid (Pareles 1985), Comic Relief, Sun City, and USA for Africa are all programs that began or occurred by the end of 1985 and served some social purpose. The integration of popular culture and cause campaigns saturated the 1980s, becoming ubiquitous features of prime-time television and mainstream public consciousness.

USA for Africa was the American rejoinder to Band Aid. Coordinated by prodigal producer Quincy Jones, Michael Jackson and Lionel Richie penned the anthem "We Are the World," communicating a latent cosmopolitanism and concern for the welfare of those suffering from malnutrition and starvation in Africa. This organization emerged after release of the song and was designed as a short-lived, but lofty, operation "to meet immediate famine relief needs in Africa, to provide necessary materials and supplies to the destitute people in Africa to enable them to become self-sufficient, to provide funds for long-term economic development…to provide emergency food, clothing, shelter and medical relief to needy people in the United States" (quoted in Scott and Mpanya 1994, 3). This description includes its domestic work, constituted by 10% of its budget, that resulted in the Hands Across America campaign to combat homelessness and poverty in the USA (Scott and Mpanya 1994, 3). From the proceeds of the song alone, in 1985, USA for Africa raised $50 million, which would rise to a single-year figure of $98.6 million by 1989, its final year of full operation (Scott and Mpanya 1994, 57). The sheer fact of having generated numbers of this magnitude from the production of one hit single is staggering and in significant ways builds on the success of previous events.

However, the famine relief campaign is a marked departure from the Amnesty events that preceded it because of its distance from political discourse. That there was a civil war raging in Ethiopia during the famine was a key fact conspicuously absent from all campaign messaging. Not only was the war occurring contemporaneously, food was also being used as a weapon of war. But in the humanitarian campaign, there is no discussion of the politics of the famine or the way in which food was being leveraged by Colonel Mengistu Haile Mariam of Ethiopia, who was engaged in battle with separatist groups from Eritrea and Tigray. Alex de Waal contends that the 1984 famine was not the product of drought at all, but that drought accentuated circumstances on the ground, namely "the bombing of markets in rebel-held areas; restrictions on movement and trade; the forced relocation of population; and finally the manipulation of relief programs" (de Waal 1997, 117).

The final element on de Waal's list is the most scandalous when considering the impact of humanitarian aid. In order to gain access to rural populations and mediate the flow of money, the United Nations Emergency Office for Ethiopia made arrangements with Mengistu and subsequently defended his policies of military bombardment and resettlement so as to certify the UN's in-country presence. "There is no doubt that this relief program supported President Mengistu militarily and politically. In Tigray, very few rural people and very many soldiers were fed by the relief. The humanitarian effort prolonged the war, and with it, human suffering" (de Waal 1997, 127). This conclusion supports a central thesis of this chapter: The absence of politics in the humanitarian campaign for famine relief permitted the warring parties to manipulate the aid relief.

As well, in light of de Waal's analysis, it is reasonable to hypothesize about counterfactuals. If the masses of supporters, who were so moved by the impassioned pleas of Geldof, Bono, and company, were all more attuned to the political realities of Ethiopia, perhaps there may have been a sustained call for an investment into a durable peace to end the war and with it end the starvation. Had the appeal been to write letters, attend rallies, and employ direct action tactics targeting elected officials, perhaps American political will could have been motivated to intervene in a sensible and meaningful way. This is one alternate history.

But this reality never took shape as the central force of campaign messaging. Instead of confronting the facts of the war, and the way in which food aid was being used as a device with which to execute a massive resettlement plan, the humanitarian movement focused on the famine and its "natural" causes. As Geldof himself writes, "This was what the concert was all about: ...hunger. About hunger, about drought, about famine. About despair..." (Hillmore 1985, 40). The central premise informing the movement was that suffering in Ethiopia was "all for want of food," which of course was true in a certain sense, but also obfuscates the actual nature of the crisis and complicated relief efforts (Hillmore 1985, 42).

When provisions began reaching Ethiopia in greater volumes as the pop culture campaign ramped up, the aid itself was strategically located and then relocated to suit Mengistu's military objectives. In order to undercut support for the rebels, he sought to move hundreds of thousands of civilians from the Tigray and Wollo regions. Not only was the resettlement program a hindrance to the distribution of food aid, but also the distribution centers were set up as a destination for those Mengistu wished to resettle; relief provisions were also withheld until after the resettlement program concluded ("Evil Days: 30 Years of War and Famine in Ethiopia" 1991). The deliberate manipulation of global humanitarian actors for the purpose of domestic counterinsurgency is an essential fact of this conflict that was lost on the Live Aid crowd. Rather than seeking a peaceful reconciliation to the conflict, and therefore easing the transfer of aid and mitigating famine conditions, the campaigners maintained a narrative that avoided political questions of power and war in favor of apolitical humanitarian neutrality.

This position relied on a specific and limited set of tactics that flow directly from this neutral assessment of the crisis: People are suffering from lack of resources; therefore, more resources will alleviate their suffering. The sole purpose of Band Aid, Live Aid, and USA for Africa was to generate money and put that money into the hands of those who could make a difference. Again, Geldof writes hoping to compel the compassionate to do more than just care: "What is needed now is more money, lots more money. That's so much more important than sympathy and sorrow" (Hillmore 1985, 46). The only modest political angle in this equation is the way in which these movements mobilized Europe, the USA, and the UK to devote national resources to the aid effort in the form of donation as well as logistics and command throughout the delivery process. Geldof, in fact, was not shy about articulating the need for state support of humanitarian efforts and engaged in a famed shouting match with Prime Minister Margaret Thatcher over the weakness of the British state response (Garfield 2004). Despite this tenacity, there does not appear to have been any call for states or civil societies to get involved with the crisis in Ethiopia politically or diplomatically—to end the war or at least to protect civilians.

Paradox of Anti-political Pop Culture Humanitarianism

Another plausible alternate reality would have been to design a campaign calling for political intervention in the internal affairs of Ethiopia for the purpose of alleviating the suffering of innocent civilians. To have done so in 1985 would have led to a clash of cold war geopolitics and would extend the West into areas that stretched or conflicted with national interest. From an advocacy perspective, this would have been a taller task and required greater commitment on behalf of supporters (precisely the kind witnessed in the movement to end Apartheid in South Africa). Due to the complexities of the political route, humanitarian neutrality permits a quick entry into the crisis and creates space for emergency response. It is not as if it was out of step to think about famine as a complex humanitarian emergency. "In 1984, the year of the big Ethiopian famine, the World Food Council of the United Nations pronounced, 'Hunger today is largely a man-made phenomenon: human error or neglect creates it, human complacency perpetuates it and human resolve can eradicate it'" (Hillmore 1985, 3). But, humanitarian movements are inherently ill-equipped for action that confronts state interest and not disposed toward challenging global structures of power, such as neoliberal capitalism (Müller 2013). Rather, humanitarianism, as a mode of ethical action in the world, folds neatly into preexisting structures and magnifies and multiplies prevailing forms of authority.

Ultimately, the humanitarian movement for famine relief designed and executed a deliberate, focused strategy: If masses of ordinary people are made to feel compassion toward suffering Ethiopians, then they may be compelled to contribute to the alleviation of this suffering; if sufficient awareness is raised about this suffering, and if sufficiently low demands are made of the audience, then overall participation and output will be high. Context and details—those that most closely and accurately mirror the truth and portray crisis in the most factual way—are sacrificed at the altar of expediency. In the process, misguided advocacy strategies drive misinformed and malignant interventions.

The paradox inherent in deploying celebrity spokespersons for humanitarian causes is clear to the audience member, forcing the presenters to continually justify their tactics. Indeed, it became a task in itself to foreground the entertainment of Live Aid, while also concentrating the audience's attention on the famine, and the concert's official communication exerts effort to emphasize how charitable the artists were in donating their time for this important cause. For instance,

> In between one of his exits, David Bowie introduces a specially made video about the famine in Africa. He decided at the last minute to drop one of his songs in favor of the video. A rock star without an ego? This day is certainly unique. After the noise, a sudden hush and stillness falls over Philadelphia and Wembley, and in millions of homes. More money is received at that moment than at any other point of the day. (Hillmore 1985, 128)

The awkward juxtaposition of egoistic rock star and desperate famine victim is ever-present in mass appeal campaigns. Why should middle-class television audiences be asked to donate small change, while these celebrities could wipe malnutrition away forever with the stroke of a pen? Bono and his wife, following Live Aid, did travel to Ethiopia to work at a feeding center, in order to allay his own "uneasiness at U2 benefitting commercially from their participation in the historic Live Aid gig" (quoted at Gill 2012, 13). This gesture notwithstanding, the class implications of the relationship constituted at the nexus of celebrity-audience-recipient demonstrates the gross inequality in wealth distribution and suggests that campaigns like this one are not terribly concerned with global economic justice. Instead of challenging unjust resource distribution, or the system of consumer capitalism that facilitates it, audience members are lulled by entertainment and celebrity seduction. With consumerism as conduit, the campaign and its adherents are limited in their ability to explore and address root causes—root causes of famine in Ethiopia, the systemic origins of resource scarcity and underdevelopment, the legacies of imperialism and colonialism, or the politics of proxy wars.

The crisis in Ethiopia galvanized the public unlike any other international humanitarian event. Utilization of benefit concerts and popular culture, and the ability for imagery and information to be communicated through new communications technology—by 1990, 56% of US households had cable television, up from 12% in 1975—provided the wherewithal for a truly mass sentiment to emerge (Nielsen Group 2009, 3). Production of the cause-song "We Are the World" signaled a new approach to marketing human rights that combined thoroughly commercial approaches to outreach with more conventional tactics.

Mobilizing the Masses to End Apartheid

By the end of the 1980s, global public consciousness around human dignity reached a crescendo with the fall of the white government in South Africa. Thirty years of transnational activism and advocacy culminated in this victory, standing on the shoulders of decades of violent and nonviolent grassroots struggle by black South Africans and allies. Because of the way the conflict extends out from the depths of the cold war into the era of global governance, the efforts to dismantle Apartheid epitomize and express concurrent geopolitical shifts. The globalization of moral awareness for the suffering of distant others helped magnify and multiply the force of domestic resistance against institutionalized racism. During the transitional period, the international community assisted in local processes with drafting a new constitution and accounting for the truth of past violations. Global civil society, in the form of nongovernmental and international organizations, stepped into the void to occupy crucial space and assert norms of rule of law, democracy, and human rights protection. As a fundamental bridge between the past and the present, the movement to end Apartheid capitalized on the broader awareness for human rights and humanitarianism described here by mobilizing mainstream publics in Western societies behind the cause of equality.

The Anti-Apartheid Movement was not a membership-based movement like Amnesty International, nor was it a donor-based campaign such as Live Aid or Band Aid. Economic tactics provided a means for advocates to leverage their consumerism in such a way that affected the politics in South Africa. Because the country was a hub of international business activity, boycott and divestment strategies were able to be effective. Furthermore, the cultural segment of the boycott movement forged a connection between the benefit concert events of the period, mass consumption, and the political imperatives of the overthrow of Apartheid. Most crucially, the coordination between transnational advocates and grassroots activists built an unmovable foundation.

The boycott component had become a global movement by the mid-1980s, spearheaded by the Anti-Apartheid Movement begun in 1959. Initially a group of South African ex-patriots and their British supporters, the Boycott Movement was from the start conscious of its potential: “When our local purchasing power is combined with that of sympathetic organizations overseas we wield a devastating weapon" (quoted in Gurney 1999, 33). The 1976 Soweto uprising accelerated such attempts as divestment campaigns sprung up in universities seeking to punish companies with business interests allied with the white government. Specific campaigns aimed at corporations such as Polaroid, Chase Manhattan, Citibank, Manufacturers Hanover, Mobil, Shell, Ford, General Motors, and IBM opposed their support for Apartheid and sought to stimulate capital flight out of South Africa (Knight 2004).

A cultural boycott took shape to leverage the visibility of public events, athletes, and celebrities. In sports, politics spilled over into international competitions including the Olympics, the Commonwealth Games, rugby, and cricket (Stevens 2013). In music, the movement raised the stakes for those offered to perform in South Africa. Those artists that violated the cultural boycott, such as Frank Sinatra, faced the scorn of their peers and fans. Those, like Roberta Flack, who turned down enormous contracts, were celebrated as vanguards (Reddy 1984). Stevie Wonder, among others, was arrested in staged protest events in front of the South African embassy in Washington, DC. The Anti-Apartheid Movement effectively penetrated a high echelon of popular culture and forcefully deployed its influence.

Following in the footsteps of the Secret Policeman's Ball and Live Aid, there were a range of cultural products that emerged to confront the white South African government over the policies of Apartheid and the continued detention of Nelson Mandela. "Sun City" was the recording project of Little Steven Van Zandt (of E Street Band fame) that brought together artists to support the cultural boycott of Apartheid South Africa and clearly had a more radical tone than did its contemporaries. Sun City is a casino, resort, and music venue located in what was then a Bantustan, and the project aimed to mobilize artists to refuse offers to perform in Sun City. Artists United Against Apartheid, the umbrella organization, was "not just an issue of solidarity with a political mass movement, but also a recognition that those involved are fighters, not simply victims" (Ullestad 1992, 49). In addition to the initial song that spanned musical genres, bringing together Public Enemy, George Clinton, Pat Benatar, Hall and Oates, and Joey Ramone, Sun City was also a music video with MTV airplay and a book geared toward educating the public on Apartheid (Ullestad 1987, 67). The Anti-Apartheid Movement rode the wave of the 1980s and follows closely in the footsteps of John Cleese and Bob Geldof.

Furthermore, on July 11, 1988, in London, a seventieth birthday celebration was held for Nelson Mandela at Wembley Stadium and broadcast worldwide to 600 million viewers. Again, with a deliberately political tone, artists took the stage to demand the release of the leader of the African National Congress (ANC) and for an end to Apartheid generally. The song "Sun City" was featured, as was "Biko," Peter Gabriel's tribute to the martyred ANC leader Steve Biko that had also been performed at Amnesty International's 1986 Conspiracy of Hope tour.

In the USA, the concert received an abbreviated and censored broadcast on the Fox Network, owned by arch-conservative Rupert Murdoch, which was edited for content and from which was removed Anti-Apartheid tirades by the musicians; incidentally, the television version was also paid for with advertising by many companies still conducting business in South Africa. The 72,000 fans in attendance at Wembley that day were treated to a dizzying array of star power that measurably raised the profile of the global Anti-Apartheid Movement. In 1990, once Mandela was released from Robben Island, another mega-event was held in London to celebrate his freedom. However, by this point, even MTV declined to air the concert because "they had already committed to airing a Muscular Dystrophy benefit shortly after the Mandela date" and could only manage one benefit broadcast in a short period of time (Garofalo 1992a, 63). This conclusive point evidences in many ways the perception of "charity rock" by the end of the period—that there was a limit to what the public and the market would tolerate with respect to cause-driven cultural events.

Most unique about the Anti-Apartheid Movement in the context of this era was its skillful blend of political and economic tools. In addition to political pressure at the UN and in domestic legislatures, the use of boycotts and divestment tactics created economic consequences for South Africa's policy decisions. These sweeping measures aimed to punish business interests tied to the rogue state. Besides the obvious point that boycott and divestment hurt the bottom line, their other primary impact was to endow ordinary consumers with extraordinary power. This introduced a great degree of democracy into the marketplace where conscious consumers could "vote" with their dollar. Effectively, citizens were able to shift the current against the white government by increasing the costs on commerce. The balance of power tilted in favor of the transnational movement as an exodus of capital continued through the end of the 1980s.

I must stress how historically contingent I believe this phenomenon to be: Due to the expansion of the society of mass consumption during this period—because of the cultural hegemony of excess, the imperative to participate in conspicuous consumerism, and the ready availability of personal finance—the moment was ripe for the advocacy community to link shopping habits of individuals to campaign objectives—smart and clever, even. Despite the seductive draw of consumer capitalism, the South African case illustrates that the reins of the market can be harnessed. With the initiation of boycotts, sanctions, and divestment as new advocacy tools, the impulses of narcissistic consumerism are directed in the service of human rights. It seems as if it is indeed possible for one to pursue one's own self-interest while creating externalities that benefit campaigns for human dignity. The final lesson learned from South Africa is that the success was based in the solidarity of global citizens alongside domestic activists endowed with precise weapons and clear goals operating in both the economic *and* political spheres. Contemporary campaigns that rely on consumers as advocates, but fail to involve themselves in political struggles, are limited in their capacity and vulnerable to the false hope in capitalism as a vehicle for progress and emancipation.

One-Dimensionality in Human Rights Practice

It is clear that new doors were opened for human rights and humanitarian action during this period. The deployment of the culture industry undeniably extended awareness about suffering in the world to enormous numbers of people. Funding for initiatives exploded as campaigns in the defense of human dignity gained mainstream popular appeal. Membership in human rights organizations rose significantly, enabling the expansion of casework for political prisoners and other issues. The channels through which human rights emerged were unique and groundbreaking. Average citizens were concerned with and invested in the human welfare of other people, strangers unlike themselves whom they would never meet. The contemporary human rights movement was constructed as a standing constituency of defenders prepared at a moment's notice to fire off a letter to a foreign head of state and rally for the protection of human dignity. This point cannot be over-emphasized: *the attempt to establish a global grassroots movement permanently assembled for the protection of human rights is a novel and crucial moment in human history and was facilitated, in part, through patterns of mass consumption.*

However, human rights advocacy during the 1980s is constituted by a tense combination of solidarity and self-indulgence. Celebrity endorsement and popular cultural events stir up public fervor for mass movements, which is not to say that these ethical commitments are disingenuous, but rather that they are mired in a wash of self-satisfying behavior. This contradiction—of self-serving and other-regarding behavior, of egoistic and empathic behavior—embodies the tension of the period.

A generational effect also played a role in the emergence of this phenomenon. As the baby boomer generation reached middle age in the 1980s, benefitting from the shifts in personal finance, they are drawn to mass consumption, while retaining the historical legacy of the 1960s. The same cross section that invested in money market funds and stocks was also engaged in grassroots struggles twenty years earlier. The same generation that rebelled at Woodstock, Stonewall, and Selma recalled their political consciousness, while being seduced by luxury consumption and materialism. For this reason, charity rock appeared with such force as the perfect synthesis of radical political culture and consumerism. Protest music and cause songs were familiar to this audience because of the impression that Pete Seeger, John Lennon, and Bob Dylan had on their cultural memory. Charity rock is a 1980s version of protest music, but on a grander stage and with explicit emphasis on the consumption as a mechanism for social change. However, charity rock is born of the era of the one-dimensional rock star—the ostentatious front man co-opted by capital and transformed into a marketing tool, a logo, a brand unto himself. The heroic image of popular musician as politically conscious artist is a dubious proposition because popular culture is no longer a realm of rebellion.

Describing mass culture as "pre-digested," Adorno evokes imagery of a mother bird ingesting, masticating, and regurgitating food for her young (Adorno 1994, 210). The young bird is the recipient of nourishing substance, but is not involved in the process of discovery, procurement, or even basic biological functions like chewing. Passive, the consumer of mass culture falsely associates spending money with the exercise of individuality and audience membership with political engagement. Therefore, what sense can we make of "charity rock" events or those popular cultural products that support human rights campaigns? If Adorno is correct, then this represents the commodification of human rights advocacy, a process that falsely satisfies political goals by locating their supposed remedy in commercial transactions. Celebrities, or "mass idols," in Leo Lowenthal's term, play a central role in this by contributing to the confusion of the audience and obfuscating complex political issues in international affairs. "The large confusing issues in the political and economic realm and the antagonisms and controversies in the social realm—all these are submerged in the experience of being at one with the lofty and great in the sphere of consumption" (Lowenthal 1984, 228).

Mass culture is a venue for human rights campaigns because of the deep, paralyzing disconnect between form and content, substance and essence. As Adorno writes, "Those who ask for a song of social significance ask for it through a medium which deprives it of social significance" (Adorno 1994, 212). Human rights advocates would be challenged to execute politically motivated campaigns without running the risk of dilution, perversion, or outright co-optation. The 1980s was a decade particularly ripe for mass culture and mass consumption due to changes in class structure, capital accumulation, and mainstream social values and therefore presents a questionable context for the execution of intense advocacy efforts.

Post-industrial capitalism is not designed to advance human emancipation; instead, it co-opts and commodifies those forces demanding change. Quoting Marcuse:

> It solves this contradiction by closing all avenues of escape, protest, refusal and dissociation, by absorbing or defeating all effective opposition, by closing itself against qualitative social change, namely the emergence of qualitatively new forms of human existence, and by suffocating the need for social change. (Marcuse 2001, 88)

Ultimately, the risks posed by the deployment of popular culture are real, but are not determinate. In the case of Live Aid, the commercial mechanism outweighed the humanitarian impulses, eliminating politics in favor of shallow sentimentality. However, in the case of Amnesty International, engineers of the movement were careful to maintain a balanced blend of political action and consumer behavior. There is no precise recipe for movement-building and campaign design attentive to the seductive dangers of mass consumption, but commodification of the kind described here is not merely an abstract accusation.

The concrete implications that arise from "commodification" suggest that locating human rights advocacy in commercialized terrain has a negative effect on the political capacity of the movement. Commodification impacts political capacity by reducing barriers to access and transforming human rights advocacy into a social practice that can be performed conveniently. On the face of it, this conclusion may seem counterintuitive: The crowning achievement of this period, from a human rights perspective, is how masses of ordinary people became aware of and involved in activism and action. By introducing pop culture tools into the strategic toolbox, human rights became a universe no longer reserved for lawyers, diplomats, philosophers, and professional advocates. By broadening the base of supporters for human rights and humanitarian campaigns, NGOs leveraged the grass roots effectively for the purposes of raising money and executing actions. However, by increasing participation, by simplifying messages, and by articulating human rights as a practice that fits with affluent lifestyles and mainstream values, the movement cultivates an image of human rights divorced from politics. Building a movement founded on convenience cultivates consumers rather than activists for whom political struggle is depicted as an entertaining pastime with quick fixes. Instead of an incremental battle waged through self-sacrifice and commitment, by challenging the exercise of power in a direct and confrontational way, convenient methods take the effort out of human rights struggle. The commodification of human rights advocacy transforms a political act into an economic transaction.

One-dimensionality for Marcuse describes the tendency for the society of mass consumption to stifle alternative visions and incapacitate transformational politics. For human rights advocacy, one-dimensionality explains two things: the inclination for Western supporters to focus their attention on foreign crisis and the propensity for mass campaigns to ignore or avoid root causes of abuse. It is often cynically asked why Americans, for instance, are more concerned with malnourishment in Ethiopia, but not in Washington, DC. Externalizing sentimentality for suffering becomes possible with popular culture, but by its very nature popular culture does not facilitate challenges aimed at one's own society. Similarly for political repression, when the Thatcher government set its aims on breaking labor unions, resistance erupted including that which was accompanied by protest songs by punk rocker Billy Bragg. However, Amnesty International supporters or Live Aid donors were not likely to draw parallels or take a side in the conflict because human rights violations were things that happened elsewhere; they were other peoples' problems, not ours. Engagement marked by one-dimensionality refuses to disrupt local power relations by projecting outrage abroad.

Finally, consumerism constrains the political capacity of advocacy campaigns from the outset by focusing on symptoms of structural abuse rather than on the structure itself. In its attempt to communicate simple messages and straightforward remedies to the audience, NGOs obscure the nature of problems themselves and obstruct the origins of abuse. When solutions are delimited by the official explanations, opportunities to address the deeper, structural tensions are in turn curtailed. Ultimately, the ready-made solutions for human rights abuse and humanitarian deprivation only address problems on the surface and do not require significant investment of time, energy, or money. These methods do not require personal sacrifice, and they do not entail compromising convenience or comfort. Securing structural change and provoking institutional transformation take time and involve challenging entrenched power, prevailing culture, and dominant social relations.

In the process of cultivating constituencies of compassion, the fledgling community for human dignity anchored its hopes deep in the machinery of mass consumption and popular culture. Of greatest concern is whether mainstream human rights advocacy was forged as a weak and insufficient response to violence and deprivation, to perpetually trot our tired tactics that fail to address the core problems—and are vulnerable to co-optation. With the advance of communications technology during and following this period, the ease and convenience of advocacy are supplemented by a growing demand to address distant suffering on television. As cries for intervention grow louder and more intense, the advocacy community struggles to crystallize emotional outrage into actionable engagement. The faulty and tenuous foundation of the human rights movement forecasts a rough road ahead, even as geopolitical space opens.

If history provided fertile ground for the emergence of constituencies of compassionate consumers, what can we expect as times change? How does human rights advocacy and the forces that shape it adapt to the charge of globalization and technological innovation? The impact of consumer capitalism does not remain confined to its simplest iteration as economic transaction, evolving to deepen its influence on the psychological impulses, social relations, and power dynamics. One-dimensionality continues to impede radical politics and slides seamlessly as new possibilities for struggle surface, while similar obstacles remain.

It is particularly with the advent of new platforms for visual media that human rights is confronted with an incredible opportunity to cultivate a transnational solidarity movement. However, the ability for audiences to see and witness atrocity in distant lands did not prove to be the watershed it was promised to be. The spectacle of suffering constructed through global media exploits and objectifies without solidifying a political community with the will and capacity to act. Instead, the spectacle becomes a vessel for powerful actors to corrupt and manipulate, in the pursuit of self-interest and at the expense of human dignity. Just as publics were galvanized emotionally during the Sharpeville Massacre in South Africa, as poignant images of dead and maimed children were splashed across front pages, the question remains not *how* one feels about such images, but what form of action can we muster in response.

Note

1. Based on this author's calculations from data in AI Annual Reports.

References

Adler, Jerry, Jerry Buckley, Jeff Copeland, Frank Maier, Elizabeth Bailey, Nikki Finke Greenberg, Holly Morris, Pamela Abramson, Tenley-Ann Jackson, and MacLean Gander. 1984. "The Year of the Yuppie." *Newsweek*, December, 14–24.

Adorno, Theodor. 1991. *The Culture Industry*. New York: Routledge.

———. 1994. "On Popular Music." In *Cultural Theory and Popular Culture: A Reader*. New York: Harvester Wheatsheaf.

Amnesty International. 1973a. "Amnesty International Newsletter." London: Amnesty International Publications.

———. 1973b. "Amnesty International Newsletter." London: Amnesty International Publications.

———. 1974a. "Amnesty International Annual Report 1974." London: Amnesty International Publications.

———. 1974b. "Amnesty International Newsletter." London: Amnesty International Publications.

———. 1974c. "Amnesty International Newsletter." London: Amnesty International Publications.

———. 1976. "Amnesty International Annual Report 1976." London: Amnesty International Publications.

———. 1978. "Amnesty International Annual Report 1978." London: Amnesty International Publications.
Barber, Benjamin R. 2007. *Consumed: How Markets Corrupt Children, Infantilize Adults, and Swallow Citizens Whole*. New York: W. W. Norton.
Beaud, Michel. 2001. *A History of Capitalism, 1500–2000*. New York: Monthly Review Press.
Biskind, Peter. 2004. *Down and Dirty Pictures: Miramax, Sundance, and the Rise of Independent Film*. New York: Simon & Schuster.
Clark, Ann Marie. 2001. *Diplomacy of Conscience: Amnesty International and Changing Human Rights Norms*. Princeton, NJ: Princeton University Press.
Coleman, Mark. 1990. "The Revival of Conscience." *Rolling Stone*, no. 591 (November): 69.
de Waal, Alex. 1997. *Famine Crimes: Politics & the Disaster Relief Industry in Africa*. London: African Rights and the International African Institute.
Ehrenreich, Barbara. 1989. *Fear of Falling: The Inner Life of the Middle Class*. New York: Pantheon Books.
Elliot, Jane. 2005. "The Nurse Who Inspired Live Aid." *BBC News*, July 1.
"Evil Days: 30 Years of War and Famine in Ethiopia." 1991. New York: Africa Watch. http://www.hrw.org/sites/default/files/reports/Ethiopia919.pdf.
Fricke, David. 1986. "Caravan for Human Rights." *Rolling Stone*, June 19.
Galbraith, John Kenneth. 1992. *The Culture of Contentment*. Boston: Houghton Mifflin Co.
Garfield, Simon. 2004. "Live Aid: The Man." *The Guardian*, October 16, sec. Music. http://www.guardian.co.uk/music/2004/oct/17/popandrock6.
Garofalo, Reebee. 1992a. "Nelson Mandela, The Concerts: Mass Culture as Contested Terrain." In *Rockin' the Boat: Mass Music and Mass Movements*, edited by Reebee Garofalo. Boston: South End Press.
———. 1992b. "Understanding Mega-Events: If We Are the World, Then How Do We Change It?" In *Rockin' the Boat: Mass Music and Mass Movements*, edited by Reebee Garofalo. Boston: South End Press.
Geldof, Bob. 1986. *Is That It?* New York: Weidenfeld & Nicolson.
Gill, Peter. 2012. *Famine and Foreigners: Ethiopia Since Live Aid*. Oxford: Oxford University Press.
Gurney, Christabel. 1999. "When the Boycott Began to Bite." *History Today*, June.
Harrington, Richard. 1986. "Rock for Rights: The Megaconcert for Amnesty International." *Washington Post*, June 15, sec. B1.
Henke, James. 1988a. *Human Rights Now!: The Official Book of the Concerts for Human Rights Foundation World Tour*. Topsfield, MA: Salem House Publishers.

———. 1988b. "Chimes of Freedom." *Rolling Stone*, October 20.

Hillmore, Peter. 1985. *Live Aid: World-Wide Concert Book*. Parsippany, NJ: Unicorn Publishing House.

Hopgood, Stephen. 2006. *Keepers of the Flame: Understanding Amnesty International*. Ithaca, NY: Cornell University Press.

Knight, Richard. 2004. "A Decade of Freedom: Celebrating the Role of the International Anti-Apartheid Movement in South Africa's Freedom Struggle." http://www.anc.org.za/ancdocs/history/aam/conference/rknight.html.

Larsen, Egon. 1979. *A Flame in Barbed Wire: The Story of Amnesty International*. New York: Norton.

Lowenthal, Leo. 1984. *Literature and Mass Culture*. New Brunswick, NJ: Transaction Books.

Marcuse, Herbert. 1964. *One-Dimensional Man*. Boston: Beacon Press.

———. 2001. "The Containment of Social Change in Industrial Society." In *Towards a Critical Theory of Society*, edited by Douglas Kellner. London: Routledge.

Martin, Randy. 2002. *Financialization of Daily Life*. Philadelphia, PA: Temple University Press.

Mason, Roger S. 1998. *The Economics of Conspicuous Consumption: Theory and Thought Since 1700*. Cheltenham: Edward Elgar Publishing.

McCall, Douglas L. 1991. *Monty Python: A Chronological Listing of the Troupe's Creative Output, and Articles and Reviews About Them, 1969–1989*. Jefferson, NC: McFarland.

McGee, Matt. 2006. "It Was 20 Years Ago Today: Remembering the Conspiracy of Hope Tour." @U2.Com, June 4. http://www.atu2.com/news/it-was-20-years-ago-today-remembering-the-conspiracy-of-hope-tour.html.

Morley, Jefferson. 1986. "Inhuman Bondage." *Rolling Stone*, June 19.

Müller, Tanja R. 2013. "'The Ethiopian Famine' Revisited: Band Aid and the Antipolitics of Celebrity Humanitarian Action." *Disasters* 37 (1): 61–79.

Nielsen Group. 2009. "Television Audience Report 2008." Nielsen Company. http://blog.nielsen.com/nielsenwire/wp-content/uploads/2009/07/tva_2008_071709.pdf.

Nocera, Joseph. 1994. *A Piece of the Action: How the Middle Class Joined the Money Class*. New York: Simon & Schuster.

Ockenfels, Frank, and Robert Tannenbaum. 1990. "Bob Geldof." *Rolling Stone*, November 15.

Odysseos, Louiza. 2010. "Human Rights, Liberal Ontogenesis and Freedom: Producing a Subject for Neoliberalism?" *Millennium* 38 (3): 747–772. https://doi.org/10.1177/0305829810364876.

Pareles, Jon. 1985. "New Africa-Aid Efforts." *New York Times*, October 1.

Power, Jonathan. 2001. *Like Water on Stone: The Story of Amnesty International*. Boston, MA: Northeastern University Press.
Reddy, Enuga S. 1984. "Cultural Boycott." January 11. http://www.anc.org.za/un/reddy/cultural_boycott.html.
Rolling Stone. 1988. "Worthy Causes." *Rolling Stone*, December 12.
Russell, Cheryl. 1993. *The Master Trend: How the Baby Boom Generation Is Remaking America*. New York: Plenum Press.
Scheinman, Ted. 2008. "The Secret Policeman's Ball(s): Martin Lewis, John Cleese, and the Origin of the Superstar Benefit Love-Fest." *Washington City Paper*, September 29. http://www.washingtoncitypaper.com/blogs/artsdesk/music/2009/09/29/the-secret-policemans-balls-martin-lewis-john-cleese-and-the-origin-of-the-superstar-benefit-love-fest/.
Scott, Michael, and Mutombo Mpanya. 1994. *We Are the World: An Evaluation of Pop Aid for Africa*. Washington, DC: InterAction.
Stevens, Simon. 2013. "Why South Africa? The Politics of Anti-Apartheid Activism in Britain in the Long 1970s." In Jan Eckel and Samuel Moyn (eds.), *The Breakthrough: Human Rights in the 1970s*, 204–225. Philadelphia, PA: University of Pennsylvania Press.
Thompson, Andrew. 2008. "Beyond Expression: Amnesty International's Decision to Oppose Capital Punishment, 1973." *Journal of Human Rights* 7 (October): 327–40.
Ullestad, Neal. 1987. "Rock and Rebellion: Subversive Effects of Live Aid and 'Sun City'." *Popular Music* 6 (1): 67–76.
———. 1992. "Diverse Rock Rebellions Subvert Mass Media Hegemony." In *Rockin' the Boat: Mass Music and Mass Movements*, edited by Reebee Garofalo. Boston: South End Press.

CHAPTER 4

The Spectacle of Suffering, Transnational Witnessing, and Solidarity

Introduction

Globalization sweeps in full of promise and potential. In its infancy, neoliberal social forces drive consumerism and egoism, and through its adolescence, the narrative matures into a grand feeling of cosmopolitan communalism. Market fundamentalism and human rights advocacy emerge as dual yet divergent expressions of individualism in a world increasingly defined by its interdependence. Technology is a prime vehicle for globalization and its visual dimensions present an essential vector through which late twentieth century-debates about self and other occur. This debate takes two forms, each with important human rights implications. Most often, the controversy revolves around the interaction between the audience's subjectivity and the subject's objectification. What are the ethical responsibilities of the television viewer toward the vulnerable individual on screen? Literature on distant suffering is robust and crosses academic disciplines freely, making it engaging and approachable. The topic also circulates through mainstream media venues regularly when Western audiences confront global crises. Content motivating this aspect of the debate may be journalistic coverage of suffering, but it is as likely to include media products of human rights and humanitarian organizations. Similar considerations apply to news outlets and NGOs:

J. R. Pruce, *The Mass Appeal of Human Rights*, Human Rights Interventions, https://doi.org/10.1007/978-3-319-92075-7_4

What are our duties? To what ethical codes are we bound? What is effective in galvanizing the audience? Technology institutionalizes this debate at the intersection of emotion, communication, and politics by insisting that audiences wrestle with their obligations to suffering strangers.

But what about the relationship among television viewers? If we all watch the same event at the same time through the same medium, do we become greater than the sum of our component parts? Is an audience truly a citizenry? Communications technology is purported to be a social epoxy, and not only across great distances. Proto-globalization luminaries claimed that the very fact that we all use the same computer operating systems was a signal that we were somehow more cohesive (Friedman 2005). Surely, still today this belief holds sway. Digital networks are supposed to bring us closer together through sharing, but not only sharing—rather, through a generalized, profound, and ethereal feeling of togetherness. From a human rights perspective, the collective experience of audiences presents an opportunity to organize, but one that is only possible with the advent of a globalized media fixated on the visual. The age of spectacle emerges as the graphic apparatus providing cultural structure to neoliberal capitalism, but it resides in a historical context that profoundly informs the human rights community to this day.

When pictures emerged from Bergen-Belsen following the Allies' liberation of Nazi-occupied Europe, Western audiences were genuinely shocked at the level of brutality that had occurred literally in their own backyard without their full knowledge (Zelizer 1998). The problem, however, was that the exposure of Nazi atrocities arrived too late. Despite comprehension of the crimes at the highest level of governments in Europe and North America, publics learned about the camps and the Final Solution only after the war was over. And while widespread doubt and denial plagued mainstream viewers even after the release of the photographs, a vocal segment of the international community pledged "Never Again" and promised that *had they only seen pictures of the piled bodies and gas chambers sooner, they would have acted to bring these horrors to a halt*. Concurrent with the adoption of the Genocide Convention and Universal Declaration, a central tenet of human rights rose out of the putrid Auschwitz smoke: Moral force and political power lie in the capacity of advocates to reveal crimes to the world, for abuse and violation fester in the shadows; criminals need only evade the public eye in order to remain safe from pressure and prosecution.

Therefore, it stands to reason, as technological capabilities for information gathering and sharing grow, human rights advocates would have more powerful tools at their disposal. While the political deployment of information remains a key method of human rights advocacy, in exploring the spectacle of suffering we encounter the upper limits of its logic. Naming and shaming as a tactic is bolstered by the capacity to expose abuse and remove the veil that protects impunity, but the strategy's functionality needs to be investigated. Because even today the human rights movement is doctrinaire in its goal of "raising awareness," a call that rings hollow given plentiful examples in which being aware of human rights abuses was clearly insufficient for stopping them. That we are now capable of seeing suffering with greater ease does not imply that audiences are simply human rights advocates in waiting. And despite the fact that this lesson is demonstrated as early as 1993, it has yet to sink in.

The "spectacle of suffering" is novel for the way it emerges during a period marked by transnational citizen advocacy in a social world structured and saturated by visuality. Scope and scale distinguish the spectacle from all its antecedents. Images constitute a spectacle not only because they are spectacular—that is, visually arresting—but also for how they signify and express a feature of a mass media environment heavily and increasingly reliant on visual devices for communication. The spectacle is a realm in which optics precede and supersede politics. How things appear to be stands in for how they are, why they are, or how they should be. The spectacle is a venue for conflict that impacts the physical world but also exists on a separate plane. She who commands the meaning and weaves the narrative through images influences real-world outcomes. If the spectacle is a space for negotiating power and claims to authority, the *spectacle of suffering* places brutalized human bodies at the center of these disputes. Global elites clamor for propriety over human objects captured by the lens and assert that it is they who justly and appropriately represent groups facing violence and indignity.

Crisis in Somalia erupts at the dawn of the contemporary age of media spectacle. The case provides ripe content with which to analyze the impact of graphic imagery of suffering on human rights advocacy because this moment should have been a watershed. For the first time, the television audience was fully positioned to constitute a standing mission of global witnesses given the ability to see suffering in real time from the comfort of their homes. Viewers were regularly presented with evidence of gross mistreatment and deprivation and coaxed along the path of moral awareness. This is a dream scenario for human rights NGOs because half of the work was already complete—the work of uncovering stories of suffering and lobbying mainstream global media outlets for coverage. The task for advocacy organizations would be to harness the audience's emotional reaction and translate it into action.

Instead of galvanizing a solidarity movement for the human rights of distant others, though, the spectacle of suffering promotes staring and gawking as if at a car crash, with onlookers interested to see what's happening but unwilling to pull over and help. Rather than witnesses, in the sense of bearing witness in defense of human rights, audiences were transformed into mere spectators. Despite the promise of the media age, the spectacle proves to be a space in which audiences are vulnerable to manipulation and co-optation. The spectacle of suffering produces a fragmented audience of individuals and obstructs attempts at collective action by its very nature.

This chapter discusses the failed promises of global mass media as a panacea for human rights. By historicizing the spectacle, twenty-first-century advocates can learn the inherent limitations of the visual as a plane for supporting movement-building. The exploration of Somalia provides a look at the state of human rights reporting in the context of the media spectacle surrounding the intervention. Discordance between human rights reporting and media coverage of the famine and war in Somalia highlights a natural rift. Finally, the chapter concludes with a critical perspective on the political economy beneath the spectacle and its impact on the potential for constructing communities of transnational solidarity.

The Evolution of the Spectacle in History

Events marked by the broad public dissemination of graphic images of suffering are well documented in history from as far back as the Lisbon earthquake in 1755, through the Napoleonic conquest of the Iberian Peninsula, and the movement to free the Congo from King Leopold II (Sliwinski 2011). Observers of atrocity discover a relationship with the suffering individuals through the process of seeing them suffer, as represented in an etching, a drawing, a lantern projection, or a photograph. When, in 1992, pictures and video streamed westward of a famine gripping rural civilian populations in Baidoa, Somalia, audiences quickly located the images in a familiar context. Most recently, the 1984 Ethiopian famine that spawned Live Aid hinged on a graphic portrayal of starvation discussed here in the last chapter. The *BBC* report that launched the relief effort for Ethiopia featured the sort of visuals that have become common ingredients in crisis reportage, particularly of malnourishment and particularly of Africa: sullen staring eyes, protruding ribs and clavicles, limp skin hanging off weak bodies, swollen bellies of protein deficient children, and mothers too drained and dehydrated to nurse their young. What the images could not communicate the voiceover assisted with, as the journalist spoke with biblical allusion and Manichean tone about the certain fate of these hopeless innocents. Through the lens of Ethiopia, Somalia is brought into focus.

But the true genesis of the iconography of famine begins long before even this period. Reluctantly, in 1960, Belgium relinquished control on its long-held and thoroughly terrorized territory in the Congo Basin. While the history of King Leopold II's personal colony has been deftly explored (Hochschild 1999), the post-colonial Congo was also fraught with dire suffering. In the chaos that ensued following the evacuation of Belgian forces, the UN, under the direction of Secretary-General Dag Hammarskjold, initiated its first peacekeeping intervention. But, on the fringes of Leopoldville, hunger set in among rural inhabitants and refugees from the violence in the capital. Late that year, the *Observer* ran a single story that catapulted the crisis into the consciousness of readers and bolstered the visibility of Oxfam, the aid organization that became most closely associated with the response through its public appeals. "People working for Oxfam at the time remember that story in the *Observer* with the clarity normally reserved for the deaths of presidents and the outbreak of war" (Black 1992, 63). For Oxfam, and the greater British humanitarian community, Congo was the event that propelled care and concern for those suffering from hunger into a mainstream position—all of which became possible due directly to the visual imaging of those Congolese famine victims.

This event initiated the icon of the starving African child in humanitarian campaigns. "The tragedy in the Congo burnt the image of the starving African child onto the collective…conscience" (Black 1992, 63). As well, NGOs learned that their success could be tied to media exposure, while newspapers learned how these images and stories captured the attention of the readers. A symbiotic relationship was forged. More outlets picked up on the story and coverage expanded, accompanied by strong photographs of human suffering. From a four-page spread in the *Mirror*, Oxfam gained promotional material and "ordered 50,000 reprints of the news spread and mailed them to all its supporter groups and donors. The coverage brought a tidal wave of response" (Black 1992, 65). Quite literally, photojournalism produced campaign material for the NGOs.

For the rest of the month of January 1961, Oxfam witnessed a lockstep rise in donations correlated to media coverage of the famine; over £100,000 rushed in directly to benefit the Congo Appeal. As newspapers continued to carry the story, and run it alongside graphic imagery, British citizens continued to give money to the cause. To supplement the coverage, Oxfam took out paid advertising appeals in dailies that reproduced the photographs (there were also a deluge of appeals that the newspapers ran at no charge to the aid agencies). Oxfam pressed on in hopes of maintaining this momentum before the story receded. A decade earlier, Oxfam accounts for £5 received for every £1 spent on advertising—this figure jumps by over six times following the campaign for Congo (Black 1992, 80). Being able to draw a straight line from graphic imagery to cash establishes clear incentive structures for strapped aid organizations.

Playing on predictable emotional reactions compelled Oxfam to prioritize the visual in its campaign communications by using images intended to make the audience "uncomfortable" and even imply a "strong hint of accusation" (Black 1992, 80). One Oxfam donor sent a note reflecting on the discomfort that these images provoke: "No child on earth should look like this" (Black 1992, 66). While perhaps a throwaway message from a sympathetic supporter, it is worth recognizing that donor's emphasis on the appearance of the child. The message could have read: "No child on earth should *live* like this." The way the child appears to the audience is ontologically prior to the way the child actually lives. The vision of suffering provided a bridge for the Western viewer to conceive of life elsewhere, but the donor's sentiment conveys a connection to that distant other that begins and ends in the process of seeing. Unconcerned by the child's actual life, the donor's appreciation for the experience of the suffering other is confined by the four sides of the photograph and does not permit a deeper exploration. In crucial ways, this neatly captures the humanitarian sensibility: The before and after of suffering matter less than what I see and do in the instant of feeling grief and pity. What causes the child's suffering or what happens after emergency relief arrives simply are not questions the humanitarian spectator asks, regardless of the jolt of the initial shock. The still image suspends a single instant with no past and no future.

Indeed, to the extent that both Oxfam and British news outlets benefited from the use of graphic images of human suffering, the Congolese children in this case were largely passive subjects. With a toehold in Western consciousness, the icon of the starving African child became a matter not only for NGOs or mass media to leverage, but one that victim groups could participate in as well. The multidimensionality of the spectacle of suffering becomes apparent as early as 1968 as the civil war in Nigeria, also known as the Biafran War, was brought into Western homes in the form of photographic evidence of the starvation of civilians among the secessionist Igbo people.

War photography by Gilles Caron of France and Don McCullin of the UK has come to epitomize the ability for an image to frame a conflict and communicate the desperate predicaments of the subjects of the photograph for an unsuspecting audience. Beginning in the spring of 1968, news of the conflict began to flow to Western news outlets through the reporting of Caron and McCullin. On May 4, 1968, Caron's photographs were published in the *Paris Match* and were thereafter syndicated in *The New York Times Sunday Magazine* (US), *Manchete* (Brazil), and *Kwick* (Germany) (Cookman 2008, 227, 238). On June 12, similar photographs were plastered on the cover of *Life* magazine and in *The Sun* (Heerten 2009, 5–6). These photographs have, over time, gained an iconic status because of their impact on the public and the way in which they have laid the foundation for atrocity coverage to follow.

The images from the region of Biafra portray the debilitating effects of chronic malnutrition on women and children. In a raw fashion, they capture the physicality of suffering by focusing the viewer's attention on the extreme toll taken on the body:

> In one, a child attempted in vain to suckle his mother's withered breast. In another, a group of naked boys stood intently watching some action... Caron focused on a boy in the front rank, gently grasping a slender stick; its thinness emphasizes the boy's wasted limbs...The other photograph shows a girl of indeterminate age, who seems little more than a tissue of skin stretched tautly across ribs and shoulders. (Cookman 2008, 238)

Effectively, the photographs break down the experience of suffering into its most visceral, human, base form in a way that translates well to an audience. Through the process of mediation, the coverage strikes at the sentimental core of the audience: "Caron humanized his subjects...gave his subjects dignity despite their suffering..." (Cookman 2008, 239).

The relationship that photojournalists hope to establish exists on the level of emotions—that viewers will respond to the way the images make them feel. Because of the nature of the still snapshot, there are many contextual assumptions that are required of the viewer that cannot be made explicit through the medium.

For instance, there is a presumption of victim innocence in the Biafra coverage. The use of women and children as subjects communicates the notion that there are powerful, external forces acting on them, due to traditional narratives of female and child passivity and vulnerability. Starvation itself is illustrated in simple terms, as a natural disaster, more akin to an earthquake than a calculated political strategy. In the case of Biafra, as well as Ethiopia, this simplicity is in fact a distortion because in both places food was being used as a weapon of war to punish civilian populations. The combination of child-like victim innocence and subsistence rights violation, beginning in 1968, casts a shadow on future incidents of visual media representation of suffering.

However, these "innocent victims" were not merely submissive subjects in the frame of the photographs—they were in fact active participants in the global trafficking of their own atrocity images. Under the leadership of Colonel Odumegwu Ojukwu, the secessionist Biafrans employed the services of Markpress, a Geneva-based public relations firm to assist in their marketing and publicity. In addition to seven hundred press releases sent to "British MPs, newspaper editors, radio and television correspondents, businessmen and academics," Markpress was more generally tasked with casting "the Biafran case in the most heartrending light" (Harrison and Palmer 1986, 22; Black 1992, 121). In the television coverage of June 12 on British outlet Independent Television News (ITN), the figure of three thousand deaths per day was quoted, despite having been drawn from "partisan" sources (Black 1992, 120–21). Ojukwu, aware of the power of the image and of the press, leveraged the "starvation card" to sway British public opinion and hopefully encourage a cessation of support for the federal government with which the Biafrans were at war (Black 1992, 121).

This proved to be an overwhelmingly successful strategy as the images of starving Biafrans galvanized British civil society and awoke a remarkable, if short-lived, movement. "Thousands of people in the west marched, protested and demonstrated, went on hunger strike, collected money, took out whole-page advertisements in newspapers and other opinion-formers" (Harrison and Palmer 1986, 34). Local "Support Biafra" committees surfaced in the UK, Belgium, France, Holland, Ireland, and the USA, and advocacy editorials appeared in major publications.

Tanzanian President Julius Nyerere quipped "If I'd been a Jew in Nazi Germany, I'd feel the same as an Ibo in Nigeria" (quoted in Harrison and Palmer 1986, 34). The British *Daily Sketch* called Biafra "today's Belsen" (Harrison and Palmer 1986, 31), a metaphor that would return once again in Bosnia in 1992. For as influential as images of famine were, they cannot be seen as neutrally filtered throughout the global mass media of the late 1960s. One party to the conflict was able to manipulate the substance to serve their own interests—although humanitarian agencies would also benefit.

Worldwide publication of Caron's and McCullin's photographs stirred the conscience of the global public and had a range of cascading effects on the NGO community. Aid agencies, such as Caritas Internationalis and Oxfam, used these images in their print advertising. Caritas literally reprinted Caron's photograph of a starving baby in their posters (Cookman 2008, 240); Oxfam, cleverly, took out ads in newspapers, such as *The Guardian*, that were reluctant to print the brutal photographs in their coverage of the crisis (Heerten 2009, 7). Famously, Biafra was the point of origin of Médecins Sans Frontières (Doctors without Borders, or MSF) when Bernard Kouchner, then a doctor on location with the International Committee of the Red Cross (ICRC), refused to maintain his silence in line with the ICRC dictum of neutrality in conflict zones. Kouchner declared the starvation an act of "genocide," imploring the world to act, and reprimanding all actors for failing to take a stance against the guilty parties in this conflict (de Montclos 2009, 71–72). The photographic evidence of the humanitarian emergency in Biafra had the effect of spurring public outcry and generating financial contributions to agencies, but also retaining simplistic storylines about the crisis, instead of delving into the political mire.

Visual mediation of the conflict brought tales of suffering to new sectors of society and, therefore, "from a media point of view, Biafra was a success story, the first major famine to be addressed through media images of starving Africans, before Ethiopia in 1984 or Somalia in 1992" (de Montclos 2009, 72). Photography brought an element of reality to viewers far removed from the crisis. Similar to coverage of the liberation of the Nazi concentration camps, Biafra shook a generation. The combination of photographs in daily papers and weekly newsmagazines, with the use of stills in the nightly broadcast news, illustrated the depths of the ongoing peril in Biafra for affluent Western classes. Biafra is important in media history because of the way in which African children specifically were featured as subjects of war photography. While many photographs had famously captured historical cases of suffering and violence—from Hiroshima to My Lai—Congo and Biafra introduced the world to African famine using a frame that would be replicated into ubiquity. Somalia brings these issues to the fore in an age of media spectacle, as well as at a transitional moment of ascendance for the human rights community.

Human Rights Reporting on Somalia

Human rights reporting typically follows a standard formula: express concern, state the problem, set the context, declare sources and methods, detail allegations, appeal to law, and call to action (Cohen 1996). Human rights advocacy groups have traditionally presented information in a straightforward, measured fashion so as to assert their credibility without appearing sensationalistic. In the early 1990s, this approach entailed the singular use of text with little or no imagery. Photographs were seen to cheapen the veracity of the research—a view that the spectacle of suffering would both challenge and verify.[1] Audiences for human rights reporting included decision makers and advocacy targets, as well as media outlets and the general public. Media operations were not sophisticated enough to parse and package information differently for distinct audiences, as they are apt to do today (Budabin and Pruce 2016). This profile of human rights reporting in Somalia demonstrates the uneasiness with the spectacle, as well as the lag of NGOs with respect to the rapid transformations in mass media. For these reasons, audiences were vulnerable to manipulation by actors with greater media savvy and clout, undermining the possibilities for solidarity.

The humanitarian community first encountered the scope of the crisis of Somalia. MSF and Save the Children, working alongside the ICRC, issued reports and press releases testifying to the rising human risk confronting people caught between boundless civil strife and a creeping famine. As fighting engulfed Mogadishu, the ability for relief organizations to deliver care diminished. MSF documents the logistical barriers to even landing planes in Somalia as early as January 1991. NGO access to the affected populations continued to wane, and makeshift hospitals and their staffs became combat targets. Shuttling between Mogadishu, Nairobi, and Mombasa, MSF workers were constantly regrouping and replenishing supplies. When nearly all other international organizations, nongovernmental organizations, and journalists fled, the few that remained became invaluable voices.

Under the duress of its mission, MSF reached out regularly to its donor bases, particularly those in France and Belgium. The communications featured first-hand accounts of the dire need for financial support so MSF could continue its life-saving efforts. Dr. Rony Brauman, then president, appealed to the public consistently and repeatedly:

> We lack neither know-how nor courage at Médecins Sans Frontières; what this team is missing is more medicines, more medico-surgical material and equipment—simply, resources. I ask for your financial support, because your donation to Médecins Sans Frontières is the foundation of our action. I will never say enough how important your gift is for us, whatever the amount. Our relief missions rely on you. On behalf of everyone who awaits our assistance, thankyou [sic]. (Médecins Sans Frontières 2013, 28)

Printed newsletters mailed to the homes of supporters consisted of typewritten text on white paper accompanied by marginal color photographs. Frédéric Laffont, a French filmmaker, was with MSF in Somalia, documenting their work for a film marking the organization's twentieth anniversary. Along with these words and images, appeals in January 1991 produced a record influx of donor cash (Médecins Sans Frontières 2013, 26). Complicating the media environment for MSF and others working to raise the profile of Somalia, the allied invasion of Iraq to repel Saddam Hussein's march into Kuwait coincided with these early accounts of complex humanitarian emergency in Somalia.

Despite major news coverage of the Gulf War and by revelations of concentration camps in the former Yugoslavia, international organizations (IOs) and human rights groups continued their alarm-sounding advocacy. In March, Africa Watch and Physicians for Human Rights released a lengthy report entitled "No Mercy In Mogadishu: The Human Cost of the Conflict and the Struggle for Relief." The report detailed the extent of the war and the scale of human devastation, discussing its research methodologies for assessing casualty figures. Citing breaches of international law for failure to distinguish civilians from combatants, all sides were urged to permit the safe passage of humanitarian relief goods. The threat of impending famine is dealt with briefly toward the end, before prescriptions are pronounced for the UN and other actors (Human Rights Watch 1992).

The text of the report itself is dry and legalistic intended for a professional audience literate in geopolitics and global norms. Human Rights Watch (HRW), then the parent organization of Africa Watch, is not known for tugging on heartstrings and this research on the crisis in Somalia marks that tradition. Insipid language, no photographs, and no data visualizations. The report barely ventures into emotive tone, avoiding personalization, speaking only in generalities about the human cost:

> The carnage inflicted upon the civilian population by indiscriminate use of weapons of extraordinary force and by the failure on all sides to abide by minimum standards of international humanitarian law (the laws of war) has already earned Mogadishu a special place in the annals of human cruelty. (Human Rights Watch 1992, 2)

At the dawn of the age of global fiber optics and live satellite feeds, Human Rights Watch remains firmly entrenched in pre-modern but battle-tested information tactics. Black ink on white paper may be fine for lawyers and diplomats, but insufficient for stirring the conscience of the mass public.

In July 1992, the International Committee for the Red Cross cited the figures of 300,000 casualties from famine since 1989, and "reiterated its six-month old estimates that 95% of the population of Somalia was malnourished" (Western 2005, 135). The United Nations High Commission on Refugees (UNHCR) "estimated that as many as 4.5 million of the country's 6 million civilians would be subject to death by starvation without some form of immediate assistance" (Western 2005, 139). While reporting from IOs does not often reach the average news consumer, inside the US administration, there were officials, such as Andrew Natsios, also advocating forcefully for intervention. Natsios, then assistant administrator of the US Agency for International Development (USAID), sought to publicize the crisis with a series of press conferences on the topic of the "humanitarian catastrophe" (Western 2005, 135). Yet, with all this discussion, there remained very little graphic coverage of the famine in Somalia. Most news outlets had pulled out due to insecurity and it was not until the Bush administration chose to make the famine an issue that media sources began covering it.

Amnesty International, in August, released its report "Somalia: A Human Rights Disaster," following an eighteen-month investigation. In it, AI presents a narrative utilizing witness testimony and poignant language to paint a picture of the human impact of the conflict. The violations revolve around extrajudicial executions and atrocities of war. Providing details on refugee vulnerability and civilian deaths, the text takes an animated form that does not simply rely on legalistic rationality. The writing trends more toward passionate prose, confronting the reader with particularities of harm to bodily integrity: Women raped, flesh bayonetted and burnt, tongues removed, limbs severed, organs lacerated, pregnancies ended, and bodies thrown into vats of boiling oil (Amnesty International 1992). Graphic descriptions of human rights abuse, departing significantly from HRW, target Amnesty's members and supporters, in addition to policymakers in governments and IOs. Still no photographs though. The only images contained in the report are a map of Somalia and a flowchart of its clan structure. Connecting style of messaging to its intended audience is crucial for understanding why these reports look so different from one another.

For Amnesty, their challenge in reporting on Somalia is twofold: That it took eighteen months to compile this report speaks to the way in which AI was not designed for crisis reporting. Particularly at the outset of a decade marred by fluid intrastate conflict, Amnesty's research arm proves itself to be incapable of reacting to emergency situations. Furthermore, despite calls from ICRC and MSF, both AI and HRW struggle to connect their human rights frame to the issue of famine. Amnesty hardly mentions it at all, while Human Rights Watch manages to appeal to the international legal prescription to provide access for humanitarian aid to civilians in conflict. Addressing epidemic levels of malnourishment and deprivation, however, remained outside of the human rights purview in the early 1990s. Human rights NGOs were forced to contextualize violations of economic rights against the backdrop of violations of the law of armed conflict and violent threats to physical security.

Physicians for Human Rights (PHR), a partner to HRW's report, releases its contribution in November 1992 focusing on the impact of landmines on the broad conflict in Somalia (to include the areas around Mogadishu, as well as the north and Somaliland). By providing an overview of anti-personnel landmines and a history of the crisis, PHR focuses attention on the methods utilized in battle, as well as their consequences. As an organization emerging from the medical community, PHR concerns itself with the anatomical damage inflicted by mines, access to surgeons and healthcare providers, and efforts toward rehabilitating survivors and removing the weapons. In 1997, Physicians for Human Rights shared the Nobel Peace Prize for its work with the International Campaign to Ban Landmines.

Again, however, the famine fades into the background of the report, in favor of political context, legal analysis, injury statistics, and a survey of available health services. While these are all presented in a reasonable and useful way, human rights reporting of the period appears detached from the media storm that surrounded Somalia by the middle to end of 1992. Distinct from research by AI and HRW, though, PHR's report was accompanied by a series of photographs taken by freelancer Peter Menzel. Menzel's photographs do not belong squarely in the category of atrocity photographs such as described above. Instead, they visually represent various aspects of the report, including experts investigating a mine site, doctors treating and interviewing survivors, and child amputees glaring upward; even the photographs of the children speak more to their survivor-ness than their victimhood.[2] Complete with maps and graphs, Physicians for Human Rights presents a dynamic report and broader communication style, even if the subject matter remains only peripheral to the scope of the conflict.

Human rights reports on the conflict in Somalia, inclusive of the war and famine, were not designed as mass appeals. Despite the distinctions among them, calls from the advocacy community were all tailored with clear purposes for specific audiences rather than broadcast for the general public. Whether the audience is Belgian MSF supporters, representatives from the African Union, or warring parties on the ground, human rights NGOs confined their messaging and communication to elite targets. Amnesty International did not even issue an Urgent Action to address any component of the crisis. The demands detailed in the reports and proclamations were not tied to citizen engagement, which prompts the question how and why did Somalia become the popular cause of the moment in the West? No major transnational human rights organizations trafficked heavily in the visual imagery that becomes synonymous with the crisis. The edifice of spectacle surrounding the situation in Somalia was driven, shaped, and capitalized upon by states, non-state belligerents, and media outlets. The lessons from Somalia teach us about the uphill battle faced by the human rights community in trying to marshal the spectacle to serve advocacy goals. Seeing is insufficient for compelling action, and this dynamic is the norm, not the exception.

Spectacle of Suffering in Somalia

For the duration of the summer of 1992, the Bush administration was mired in calls from all sides to intervene somewhere: either in Somalia or in Bosnia. Photographs of concentration camps in Bosnia had surfaced and the human rights community demanded action. Facing pressure from a range of external and internal sources, the Bush administration ultimately executed the proverbial bait-and-switch, acting in Somalia and distracting from Bosnia.[3] On August 14, President George H. W. Bush authorized a military airlift of food aid to the Gulf of Aden, as well as support for the Pakistani officers representing the UN security force. "The decision to launch the airlift to Somalia did divert media and liberal attention away from critical coverage and commentary on Bosnia and to sympathetic stories on Somalia" (Western 2005, 163). Seizing this opportunity, the USA believed it could be seen to be acting in a noble way, while in reality seeking to evade moral and legal obligations to respond to genocide in the Balkans. Optics matter in the age of spectacle: appearing to act can be as meaningful as acting at all.

With the USA engaged, from late summer 1992 through the fall, Somalia was *the* humanitarian story covered by all Western outlets. "Television and the print media were on the spot sending wrenching stories back to the United States. Stories on and photographs of the famine's victims, heroes and villains became ubiquitous" (Moeller 1999, 137). Pleads for further and more sustained action occupied the editorial pages, as calls escalated from aid delivery to a more extended presence and a revised set of rules of engagement. Philip Johnston, President of CARE-US, issued vocal calls until the "drumbeat for intervention reached its crescendo" (de Waal 1997, 185). In September, US Marines were deployed to support the airlift mission, prompting newsmagazines and various outlets to carry stories with graphic imagery of starving children. Media sources responded to the policy decision by explaining to the public why the government was taking this action. The explanation revolved solely around famine relief, saying little about the ongoing conflict or geopolitical preferences. At this point, relief organizations and the White House were carrying the narrative, satisfying their mutual interests.

In October, UNICEF (United Nations Children's Fund) Goodwill Ambassador Audrey Hepburn spent four days in Somalia, touring feeding centers and visiting with affected children. Hepburn held this post from 1989 up to her death in 1993, traveling widely in places including

Turkey, Ecuador, Bangladesh, Vietnam, Sudan, and Ethiopia to bring attention to UNICEF's work on behalf of children. In addition to these appearances, Hepburn testified before US Congress, regularly hosted benefit concerts and gala events, and participated in a variety of UNICEF fund-raising activities. The photographs that emerged from her trip to Somalia portrayed her time with malnourished children with typical but effective tropes and helped cultivate the story of the famine within the Western audience.

Images presented children with bulging rib cages, looking scared and frail. In one photograph that was repurposed as a UNICEF appeal advertisement, Hepburn carries a sunken child draped in tattered cloth, clutching at Hepburn as if for help. A consistent feature of humanitarian communication, the mother–child trope, relates as much to the audience's relationship with their own mothers as it does to the Madonna and baby Jesus. Hepburn's gestures are prominent, as a determined, outward glance or a sweet, hopeful smile. The photographs capture Hepburn in various engaged poses: holding hands, locking eyes, kneeling, spoon-feeding, and walking or sitting among large groups of children. As a full vision of the humanitarian celebrity emerged in the 1980s, famine iconography evolved to include the star or starlet positioned alongside the starving child. Audrey Hepburn projects a stark contrast in her Lacoste polo shirt and pleated khaki pants, but expresses a genuinely humane sentiment of being present, caring, and helping.

UNICEF facilitated the relief effort by funneling resources to NGOs on the ground. As well, UNICEF assisted the Bush administration by providing ideological support for the military's operations. During her stay, Hepburn flew with the US military stationed offshore as part of President Bush's airlift. Later that year, in December 1992, now sick with cancer, the historic movie star was awarded the Presidential Medal of Freedom, the highest honor given to civilians by the US government. The symbiotic relationship between private and public actors tilted noticeably in favor of state power. As in the case of Ethiopia, efforts to protect human dignity are often vulnerable to manipulation, this time through mass media, as a byproduct of the spectacle, with a direct impact on political decision making.

Hepburn was not alone. Somali supermodel Iman returned to her homeland in December, twenty years after her family left as refugees. With a *BBC* documentary crew following her, and subsequently reported in the first person for *Vogue* magazine, the project was intended "to give pain a face" (Iman 1992). The story recounts the preparation, trepidation, and anticipation ahead of the trip, and the profound experience she had while visiting. The *Vogue* essay contains photographs of children in Baidoa relief centers, including one with Iman by their side. Her prose is intimate and captures biographical background and deeply emotional content. Relative to much of mainstream writing on the crisis, Iman's reflections are lyrical and inspired (bordering on clichéd), vividly communicating her relationship to the conflict and the suffering:

> As Somalia's famine deepens, I realize the only thing that's being fed consistently is resentment...my memory stubbornly insists on the glory that Somalia once had. As we ascend in the plane that will take me back to my adopted country, the United States, I look down into the villages, and finally to sea. I shed a few tears for me, and an ocean for Somalia. (Iman 1992, 313)

The piece concludes with a list of relief agencies readers can donate to, despite the fact that the efforts had by then nearly stalled.

On December 4, President Bush addressed the nation on television to announce a surge of troops. US military was being sent to support a new, unprecedented Security Council resolution that invoked Chapter VII of the UN Charter to permit the use of force to secure the delivery of humanitarian aid. Due to rising instability in Mogadishu, the provisions that sat on naval carriers offshore could not reach relief stations. Theft and violence were rampant. Aid workers could not be adequately protected. Bush opens with a reference to the visuality of the conflict: "Every American has seen the shocking images from Somalia" (Bush 1992). To rally domestic support for his policy, Bush leverages the emotional response among the public that his government was responsible for fostering. The spectacle of suffering in Somalia permitted the USA a free hand to pursue its political preferences under the guise of humanitarian action. Rather than serving as a moral force for human rights, the act of witnessing was co-opted by the state, retrofitted to suit its hegemonic interests.

Slowly though, over the course of the fall season, the storyline shifted from the starving children and life-saving relief workers to the jingoistic vision of the US troops confronting the thuggish locals. The stereotypical portrayal of Somali combatants is distilled in the image of 0.50 caliber machine guns perched in the back of a pickup truck (or "technical"), roaming dusty streets, manned by young fighters. Juxtaposed with the properly outfitted American soldiers, the opposition appears slapdash and ill equipped, while remaining unpredictable and threatening. Journalists continually stressed that the intervention was a humanitarian mission without military objectives. "Warlords" were to blame for the inability of relief agencies to reach starving civilian populations, so the US military were called upon to carve out safe space. The Savages–Victims–Saviors complex constructed the dominant narrative justifying the intervention and the media spectacle produced the visuals to match (Mutua 2001).

To report on the imminent appearance of US forces, major news outlets followed this narrative closely. The day ahead of the landing, Tom Brokaw recorded his broadcast for NBC Nightly News from Somalia ("Famine Amongst War in Somalia" 1992). The segment opens with an introduction from Brokaw, then cuts to imagery of women and children laying around listlessly, drained of the energy required for sitting up. Video of hospital medics attending to the sick and of caregivers weighing malnourished infants on makeshift scales transitions the arc from vulnerable people to relief workers. Save the Children is recognized for its services at a nearby feeding center. Brokaw sits on the floor, commenting about the need for short-term relief but the complexities of a long-term political solution to the conflict. Finally, Brokaw throws back to the studio for details from Pentagon correspondent Fred Francis on the operational side of the mission, including parameters of the rules of engagement.

On December 9, Marines landed on the shores of Mogadishu greeted by journalists and cameras (estimates range between 75 and 300 news personnel present). The Pentagon arranged for these media representatives to be on site by issuing invitations, even positioning them appropriately (Moeller 1999, 143; Keenan 2004, 440). Deliberately evocative of the landing on Normandy Beach in World War II, the Somali expedition was designed to be a display of American power and intentionality. In the early post-cold war period, this supposedly controlled environment was a fertile context in which to make such a pronouncement, and the initial events were mediated to an extreme so as to message the event clearly to enemies and allies alike.

A 4 AM landing in Somalia provided convenient coverage for the primetime nightly news for east coast viewers in North America. Television coverage featured Christiane Amanpour's running play-by-play of the operation, live footage of night-vision camera technology, and bizarre interviews with Marine officers. As they exited vessels onto the shore, Marines were met with popping camera flashes and boom mics. The paparazzi of the humanitarian spectacle captured the moment as if an A-List celebrity was getting out of a limousine at a Hollywood premiere. Literally surprised by the greeting, the officers questioned how the presence of video cameras and floodlights might compromise the strategic advantage of a night landing. However, the strategic advantage of the media's presence was not aimed at the Somali militants, but at American viewers.

Furthermore, contrary to prevailing tales of military heroism, disembarking from naval vessels and helicopters does not make for great television. There was little resistance to the landing. Cameras did not record a live firefight, but a slow, carefully executed transport of troops into Somalia. The correspondents struggle to accentuate the drama of the event, at times rattling off each step like items on a grocery list. The news anchors bounced from pundit to pundit grasping for opinions or perspectives to heighten the sense of importance of an otherwise mundane exercise.

Ted Koppel of ABC News wandered through the Marines later that day to glean a sense of magnitude of the intervention from the officers' perspectives asking them plainly, "What happened today?" ("U.S. Marines Land in Somalia" 1992). Of the men he speaks with, many are visiting a developed country for the first time and remark on the abject inequalities between what they have in America and what they see in-country. Many describe the strategic accomplishments of the landing, including setting up a perimeter and gaining a foothold in an area with few militants. A general sentiment among group suggests a strong sense of pride in their mission and in their country for providing humanitarian aid to those who so desperately needed it. Koppel mentions at the outset that he would ask the same penetrating question to journalists and Somalis, but only Marines make the cut that was aired. Young Somali boys jump around behind interviews in progress, ogling the camera and joking with the soldiers. The Marines quoted communicate a calm demeanor, without visible fear or anxiety, with an air of confidence in their mission and certainty of success.

Yet, while the landing itself failed to generate tremendous drama on the ground, global audiences were riveted as coverage of the landing boosted television news ratings to their highest since the 1991 Gulf War (Moeller 1999, 143). Public opinion of the intervention was extremely favorable, with 81% supportive of the mission from a moral position and 70% willing to sacrifice American blood and treasure for the cause (Moeller 1999, 145). The spectacle of Somalia had shifted from the suffering other to the heroic self in a way that resonated with the audience and generated support for the Bush administration's goals. Media outlets reaped profits through an increase in television viewership and print sales. Humanitarian NGOs experienced a significant uptick in donation and publicity. The capacity for the conflict to satisfy diverse interests suggests a unique convergence of commonly antagonist parties: Neither media sources nor NGOs questioned or challenged the government's policies, while the government brought both along in tow as useful proxies. But the honeymoon phase would not last long. The spectacle of suffering is not merely a one-way device or blunt object with which to coax and compel the audience; rather, it is a co-constituted space in which meaning is shaped by multiple actors seeking to project power through modes of visual representation.

By early 1993, with the end of drought and resumption of the rainy season, the famine was effectively over, making it a "straightforward task to declare victory over starvation" (de Waal 1997, 185). However, instead of a graceful exit, the mission devolved to respond to ongoing events, and by the summer aid delivery was no longer the force's reason for being. Due to attacks against Pakistani peacekeepers, the Security Council issued another resolution permitting the use of force for the maintenance of peace and security inside Somalia. In this case, the terms meant capturing General Mohamed Farrah Aidid and disarming his troops. Because of the consistent emphasis of the media on the humanitarian nobility of the mission, this shift did not permit the continuation of the initial narrative. Instead of simplistic explanations that readily accompany humanitarian action—good/evil, hungry/food—the new objective effectively redirected the military to conduct a complex police matter in a country nobody knew anything about.

In subsequent months, the intervention escalated and chased an endlessly moving target. In the process, civilians were killed and buildings destroyed in the dense urban environment. Infamously in the fall of that year, American forces faced significant opposition from Aidid's forces. On September 25, a US helicopter was downed in Mogadishu followed by two more on October 3. The second attack resulted in eighteen US Army Rangers killed, one taken captive, and one of the bodies of the deceased dragged through the streets by children. Young Somalis danced and celebrated around the charred corpse, dangling dog tags of the dead in front of Western television cameras. Aidid played a savvy media game. Understanding the presence of global outlets and recognizing how American domestic support was essential to continue the operation, the spectacular attacks on US forces were intended to trigger a political reaction in Washington.

Fallout from the transmission of the fierce battle and brutal treatment of American casualties was immediate and dramatic. President Bill Clinton pledged a withdrawal of American troops from the UN mission in direct response. Graphic imagery of suffering had provoked a change in foreign policy, but the suffering subjects in this case were not African children, but American servicemen. While thousands of Somalis were dead or wounded when the dust settled in Mogadishu, their suffering was cast aside. Concern for vulnerable Somalis ended at the precise moment when the mission compromised national self-interest. Contrary to globalization's highest aspirations, American lives are worth more to Americans than Somali lives. Human rights universalism does not extend to the dignity of the distant stranger and certainly not in a case when trade-offs are necessary: provincialism rules, even in an era of globalized media and transnational advocacy.

The spectacle is not a useful vehicle for witnessing and solidarity. The spectacle fabricates a whole where there are only parts. And, as parts, mass grief and mass outrage are merely fleeting emotional expressions not adaptable into collective political engagement. Each audience member reacts to what he sees on television and the common responses cultivated with graphic images give the illusion of totality. As such, the spectacle is incapable and ill equipped for sustaining action in defense of human dignity. And more so, the spectacle of suffering is a duplicitous veil in which solipsism and spectatorship masquerade as displays of social cohesion. Acts of witnessing undertaken through the spectacle crystallize viewers in their individualities and impede movement-building. This dynamic serves the advantages of states, belligerents, and corporations who capitalize on an atomized audience and pursue their own narrow objectives without resistance.

Human rights reporting in the early 1990s appears out of step with the media spectacle of the period, analog in an age of digital. Communications operations expand over the course of the decade in a constant game of catch-up to utilize advances in information technology and bring traditional strategies to bear in new ways. But the human rights movement did not internalize the lessons of Somalia. Advocacy campaigns persistently attempt to generate the level of attention associated with spectacle, often deploying grave images of suffering so as to reawaken the audience's cultural memory. However, Somalia teaches us that it is not that simple. It is not a matter of more skillfully manipulating the spectacle. The spectacle of suffering is inherently flawed as the technological and visual manifestation of neoliberalism. The properties associated with the spectacle's roots in post-industrial capitalism sufficiently circumscribe its usefulness as a platform for cosmopolitan acts of solidarity for human rights protection.

Examining the Origins and Impacts of Spectacle

Manifestation of spectacle in the post-cold war period is the product of a set of parallel and interrelated developments associated with globalization: transition to a knowledge-based economy and the growth of a networked society. A series of rapid transformations swept over the world in the early 1990s, while observers attempted to frame this new epoch and understand its impact on daily life. A sense of proximity and connectedness enveloped a broad range of social spaces, from the economic sphere to cultural concepts and political organization. However, the profound effects experienced as much by peripheral societies relative to the core, as by the whole of international society itself, were not random or coincidental, but rather the result of a long process of scientific investigation, policy deregulation, and commercial enterprise.

Facilitating this shift, an infrastructure of fiber optic cables, satellites, online bulletin boards, and corporate media outlets formed an enmeshed global network. Through these channels, activity traveled instantaneously across great distances at low costs. Finance became mobile; supply chains were rerouted through new points; and migrant and contingent labor provided the workforce for the new economic environment. With mass production shifting locales from North to South, a knowledge-based economy materialized in the developed world. Labor increasingly concentrated outside the confines of trade unions and under the direction of consolidated multinational conglomerates. In place of the Fordist assembly line, the post-industrial economy is outsourced, disaggregated, and underscored by its provision of services and reliance on information technology. Instead of factories, subcontracted freelance workers began terms in cubicles, employed on a temporary basis. Markets of production and consumption emerged in places previously out of reach. In the Network Society, "informationalism... subsume[s] industrialism as the dominant technological paradigm" (Castells 2004, 8), prompting deep social and cultural shifts.

Globalization's promise expresses a profound and collective hope in technology and neoliberal capitalism. A sense of connectivity and shared purpose absorbs the anxiety provoked by the dissolution of the global order and the reintroduction of chaos and uncertainty. The dawn of a new information age made it feel as if borders actually mattered less, marginalizing nationalism in favor of regional alliances and cosmopolitan sensibilities. With interstate conflict suppressed, ethnic violence spiked as a consequence of the loosening of Soviet and American reins put in place during the long deep freeze. The newly empowered international community, driven by Western interests and resources, lurched to the rescue espousing universalist doctrines of democracy promotion and human rights protection.

Legitimized by the mainstreaming of dignity discourse that bubbled up in the 1980s, global publics rallied behind these efforts. If the individuals suffering on television possess the same inherent value as we do, then how are our obligations to their welfare best expressed? In the context of the atomizing force of late industrial capitalism—with the erosion of civil society organizations, organized labor, and traditional religious institutions—conceptions of supranational communalism and transnational equality filled the void. However, it is essential to investigate the validity and sustainability of these ephemeral attitudes. For instance, how does this outlook inform politics and policy? Indeed, for this reason, critically exploring the media through which this perspective took shape, in which the local was displaced by the global, will provide insight into fortitude of 1990s techno-utopianism.

Television is the technological medium that ushers in globalization and personifies the perception of commonality among the global audience in the early 1990s. From a twenty-first-century perspective, the Internet is the quintessential globalizer, but after the cold war, the television captured the imagination of the masses with instantaneous transmission of moving images across cable networks and satellite constellations. Innovations in communications technology and corporate consolidation of media ownership permitted uniformity in broadcast, as global viewers shared contemporaneous visual experiences. While television itself was not a novel technology, having made inroads through Western affluent classes in the 1950s, during the 1980s the medium reached across classes in the West and began to diffuse more broadly.

Spectacle on television is born of mass access combined with centralization in production, as the graphic image rises as the prevailing platform for communication. However, visuality alone does not suffice to explain the emergent spectacle; the nature of media coverage itself had taken a spectacular turn and initiated a spiraling fusion of news and entertainment. Due to competition on cable networks for viewership and advertising dollars, sensationalism drove newsgathering. Newsworthiness becomes that which attracts the largest audience, rather than being driven by relevance or necessity. Therefore, the historic divide on television between hard news and entertainment begins to erode, creating space for the hybrid version we are left with today—in which it is difficult for a viewer to decipher where the categories begin and end.

Late twentieth-century media culture highlights the extreme, the perverse, and the absurd. Events ranging from the OJ Simpson Trial and the Super Bowl to the impeachment of Bill Clinton and a Michael Jordan slam-dunk typify the context for spectacle (Kellner 2003). Even the death of Princess Diana was transformed into spectacle, with the paparazzi covering the car crash and subsequent controversy, as closely as the royal funeral and the international grieving that followed. Mass event and scandal reign, squeezing out social significance. Saturation of the airwaves with information of little consequence gives the impression that what is featured on the nightly news is newsworthy—thus beginning a perpetual feedback of hype and aggrandizement. In the spectacle, "tabloidized infotainment culture is increasingly popular," which has a negative feedback impact on events and issues that *actually* demand attention (Kellner 2003, 1). As media culture is increasingly shaped by spectacle, the irrelevant is elevated as relevant, while pressing issues become mired amidst a fog of the odd, the gratuitous, and the intriguing. When violent conflict and natural disaster are transmitted through the same channels and in the same manner as sex scandals and celebrity controversies, audience receptivity is ripe for confusion, alienation, and apathy.

This is still not saying enough, though, because it is not only news or the perception of news that is affected by spectacle, it is indeed the spectator himself. Media spectacle "describes a media and consumer society organized around the production and consumption of images, commodities, and staged events" (Kellner 2003, 2). The claim here is that spectacle is the consequence of an advanced capitalist system that seeks new realms of colonization through which to exert social control. In this context, audiences are vulnerable to manipulation and likely to support a war that serves material or geopolitical interests, but not their own. The spectacle is hegemonic in a Gramscian sense in the way it communicates the particular demands of the powerful as if they are universally beneficial. The spectacle is a venue in which meaning is constructed and contested, and the truth-value of what is presented on screen is up for grabs.

Famously, in 1991, Jean Baudrillard asked whether or not the Gulf War was "really taking place" (Baudrillard 2008b). Cable News Network (CNN) carried the war with night-vision video of missiles coasting through the air as if in a video game. Bombed out tanks littered the road from Kuwait City, and concrete rubble lay piled where buildings once stood, but shockingly little footage of actual people. No wounded, no maimed, and no dead Americans or Iraqis. The mediation of distant conflict peels away layers of reality. If the representation of war is effectively kept clean, then its executors have full latitude to operate. When US Marines were dragged through the streets of Mogadishu two years later, the bubble burst, introducing a scenario whose reality could not be filtered or spun.

Because the audience comes into contact with the world through a shadow of reality, public opinions become easily manipulated. A sanitized rendition of the ugly affair of war has the effect of numbing the audience to the terror of combat and its horrific effects. The "zero casualty" policy put in place after Black Hawk Down remains in place today (Dauber 2001). This is notable in the wars in Afghanistan and Iraq, in which the public was not subjected to the realities of the conduct of war and only recently were the news media permitted to cover the return home of flag-draped caskets. Sheltered from war's worst effects, the enterprise is located firmly in the realm of fiction. Watching crises unfold on television situates them alongside romantic sitcoms, hospital dramas, and game shows, creating an opaque media environment in which to form judgments or level critique.

Forging Transnational Solidarity

From a human rights perspective, the central question remains: What is the impact of graphic imagery of suffering on the capacity to foster and mobilize a movement in defense of human dignity? In the context of the spectacle, this question demands a critical approach to the very assumptions that underwrite transnational human rights advocacy. If solidarity is a social practice contingent on the expansion of communities of mutual support, then transnational solidarity bears an even higher threshold because in order to form these communities, distances and diversities must be transcended.

One popular globalization narrative proclaims that our ability to visually experience events simultaneously across the same platforms builds a unity among the audience that was previously impossible (Friedman 2005). In this way, a form of cohesion may be built among classes of people who share similar reactions to witnessing graphic imagery of suffering. This feeling provides a foundation for translating emotional responses into action. NGOs (and states, for that matter) leverage this shared private experience for use in public engagement campaigns and mass appeals. Watching the same news coverage and passing the information through common moral filters about the innocence of women and children, for instance, a palpable bond can be forged.

This is not an unreasonable way of thinking about the social effect of spectacle. Consider a Monday morning water cooler conversation. Co-workers banter about Sunday night television drama, maybe a reality show, exchanging reflections on the events of the previous evening that each of them viewed from their own homes. A kind of community is built around "appointment television": Shows that compel audiences to set aside specific time to watch an episode as it airs, because being a part of the initial broadcast is itself part of the experience. Marketers attempt to magnify this today with supplementary communities in social networks and online platforms ("second screen experiences"). Even if a person watches the episode from her couch on Sunday night by herself, she is not alone. Indeed, she is acutely aware of a broad national audience of which she is a part and can now even communicate with other viewers in real-time online. By time Monday morning rolls around, she will be eager to contribute to the water cooler chat. Television is a social medium in that it impresses upon the viewer a sense that even in the singular solace of its glow, she is with others. Atrocity functions in a similar way.

However, as an outgrowth of consumer culture, the spectacle nurtures selfish individuals even and especially while presenting the illusion of collectivity and solidarity. The visual becomes a zone of contradiction where, despite the essential focus on appearance, nothing is at it appears to be. As Guy Debord expresses eloquently, "spectators are linked solely by their one-way relationship to the very center that keeps them isolated from each other. The spectacle thus reunites the separated, but it reunites them only *in their separateness*" (Debord 1983, sec. 29). Audiences feel as if they are a part of a consolidated whole, yet remain apart.[4] In fact, the spectacle keeps individuals apart by reinforcing the ideology introduced by the neoliberal marketplace. Undercutting cohesion in the physical world, the spectacle displaces "lived experience…[and] supplants social participation, and new forms of alienation induce social atomization at a more abstract level" (Gotham and Krier 2008, 157). By providing an alternative plane on which viewers can be alone but feel as though they are a component of something larger, individuals are actively engaged in behavior that inhibits precisely the type of organization necessary for a solidaristic human rights movement.

Often critique of the spectacle relies on the argument that visual distraction "stupefies social subjects…[through] separation passivity, for in submissively consuming spectacles one is estranged from actively producing one's life" (Kellner 2003, 2–3). Careful to avoid overly deterministic language about the degree of self-consciousness/self-deception within the viewer, I suggest that acquiescence and participation in spectacles is a willful act rather than the product of a conspiratorial duping. Indeed, as viewers watch atrocities on television and absorb the human gravity of crisis, there is a compulsion toward associating the act of looking as a form of intervention. Instead of considering effective ways to act to resolve the suffering on television, simply by knowing and seeing, audiences are absolved of any greater moral responsibility. Human rights dogma supports false solidarity in the spectacle by emphasizing the importance of knowing and seeing, while any true transformation demands engagement and commitment that exceeds mere spectatorship. The spectacle of suffering is cultivated as much by a reluctant audience as it is by a budding advocacy community.

From the position of a major transnational NGO, audience members are equivalent to signers of a petition or percentage points in a public opinion poll: anonymous masses to be exploited for the sake of advocacy, but not put to work directly for the issue. NGOs can appeal to these masses of supporters to legitimize their work but are regularly utilized as means to an end rather than an end unto itself. Failing to build communities of solidarity is a major shortcoming of the advocacy sector and can be explained by its reliance on spectacle. Audiences before the spectacle, like consumers in a post-industrial market, confront profound forces of alienation that funnel individuals away from social relationships of cohesion and meaning. If the atomizing force of media spectacle is to be overcome in favor of coherent communities of solidarity, knowing and seeing will have to be injected with a strong dose of acting and belonging. A human rights movement constituted by individuals bound together by little more than shallow emotions and television addictions is not much of a movement at all.

Solidarity can also stretch out from the West, breaking the fourth wall and extending moral recognition to the human subjects captured in imagery of suffering. Constructing communities of solidarity requires audience members to attribute human dignity to the vulnerable on screen and acknowledge a deep degree of sameness in them. Observers regularly dismiss this out of hand by describing graphic images of suffering as "pornography of war," "pornography of violence," or "disaster pornography" (Baudrillard 2008a; Mamdani 2007; Omaar and de Waal 1993). Referring to the visual experience with distant suffering as pornographic suggests there is a prurient and even erotic sensation attached to it in the way it serves to gratify the viewer. There also exists a latent argument about exploitation when these descriptors are trotted out, as if the viewer gains pleasure from watching the subject in an intimate position (often without clothing or with little clothing), and the subject has not consented, is not being justly compensated, or is inherently unequal in some way. In this context, how can we examine the variable of dignity in atrocity photography? Is it or can it be present in a sufficient amount to serve as the basis for a relationship of solidarity? Can objectification be avoided in the process of looking?

To take seriously critical theory of the spectacle is to understand how the concept emerges as a post-Marxist critique of mass consumption. Again, Debord:

> The first stage of the economy's domination of social life brought about an evident degradation of being into *having*—human fulfillment was no longer equated with what one was, but with what one possessed. The present stage…is bringing about a general shift from *having* to *appearing*. (Debord 1983, para. 17)

Individuals devalue their own happiness and pursuit of their self in exchange for material possessions and, now, for the sake of participating in a social snare revolving around outward appearance. Individuals living in an age of spectacle consume images as they do luxury goods, at their own expense, chasing a vision of life imposed by ideology.

Visual images stand in as new kinds of shiny objects capturing, constructing, and reproducing projections of reality for the audience. Dangling and dazzling, graphic representations draw attention to new concepts and unfamiliar issues but confront the viewer as fabrications across alienated space, without the potential for direct engagement and internalization. When those dangling images are human beings, the spectacle may have the consequence of introducing viewers to distant suffering others but does so in a way that inhibits the full recognition of dignity across the airwaves; therefore, the spectacle prevents the formation of solidarity relations. In their place sits a void, a vulnerability to manipulation by actors seeking to capitalize on weak ties. It is beholden to those who purport to defend human dignity to step into the void and assert propriety over the content of the images.

Watching and being watched is an inherently non-reciprocal, one-way exchange. Somalis are not witnesses to the suffering of communities in Dayton, for instance. Such an expectation would be unrealistic. Witnessing does not flow upstream. Rather than providing a platform for the recognition of shared humanity as the basis for a cosmopolitan politics of equality, the spectacle of suffering amplifies alterity. Furthermore, spectacle transforms the subject on screen into an object. Reifying suffering posits human dignity as a thing to be consumed through the act of looking; the spectacle "is a conceptual extension of the phenomenon of reification, a process of 'objectification' or 'thingification' of social relations" (Gotham and Krier 2008, 159). Assigning roles and embedding actors with varying degrees of power ensure the promise of globalization goes unfulfilled, dashing the hopes for an emancipatory and participatory witnessing. Observing the moral gap between those on the couch and those on the screen, media spectacle permits an entry point for actors seeking to exploit the discrepancy.

This space provides an opening for the humanitarian sensibility to take root. Based in Christian ethics of charity and salvation, humanitarianism relies on inequality—for those with resources to give in support of NGO operations that assist those without. Humanitarian action does not question the distribution of wealth, nor does it inquire after the causes of complex emergencies. The iconography of famine details a history of humanitarian NGOs leveraging audience guilt or sadness for starving Africans, but never asks for an expression of solidarity with the individuals on television. Ostensibly, solidarity is antithetical to charity in that it demands a deeper moral bond that translates to a commitment to political action. However, if humanitarians were the most manipulative actors in this scenario, we would have to work to do, but the situation would be tolerable or even useful.

Of greater concern is the way in which states and belligerents utilize the media spectacle for ends opposed to the preservation of human dignity. In the case of Somalia, the Bush administration acted so as to be seen as a government that cares and through its caring could exert its strength. As well, of course, being seen to care in Somalia was also a smokescreen to distract from Bosnia—a more complicated crisis with graver stakes and built-in legal obligations to act to prevent genocide. To nuance the critical argument, it is not that the USA acted in a purely Machiavellian fashion in Somalia. Evidence suggests that President Bush and the First Lady felt grief for the famine victims, connecting the issue to their own first-hand experience in Sudan and Ethiopia during the 1980s, and deployed American power to secure for the president a humanitarian legacy. The crux of the critique of state power and the spectacle of suffering lies in understanding the spectacle to be a venue for contestation, not simply a neutral venue for transmission of atrocity photographs. As power and interest are negotiated in mass media, solidarity is stifled and dignity is objectified. Contrary to human rights dogma about bearing witness, seeing is an insufficient and dangerous substitute for acting and as such becomes susceptible to co-optation.

Bearing Witness in an Age of Spectacle

The spectacle of suffering that emerged in the 1990s is a latter-day continuation of trends in visual media communication, but in a heightened state. Technology made it possible for distant suffering to be a regular feature of nightly news broadcasts and introduced average viewers to extraordinary situations. For Western audiences, to witness suffering at a distance is to be involved in a central human rights process traditionally reserved for relief workers, medical personnel, and staff on the ground in conflict zones. From a human rights perspective, witnessing is a political act because it disables the abuser from operating in secrecy; accountability for gross violations can only occur when the veil has been lifted: "a fundamental axiom of the human rights movement in an age of publicity: that the exposure of violence is feared by its perpetrators, and hence that the act of witness is not simply an ethical gesture but an active intervention" (Keenan 2002, 446). To reiterate Amnesty International's founding motto: "Better to light a candle than curse the darkness." It is no coincidence that in 1992 the Lawyer's Committee for Human Rights began its WITNESS program that distributes video cameras throughout the world to capture human rights abuse for documentary purposes (this program was initiated by rock star/activist/Amnesty supporter Peter Gabriel) (Cohen 2001, 186). The spectacle is equivalent to the lighting of a million candles but transforming ordinary people into witnesses through television does not transform them into human rights advocates.

Yet, there is a qualitative difference between the new form of witnessing underwritten by the spectacle of suffering and those customary in the field of human rights. Witnessing from the vantage of one's living room and witnessing from within a refugee camp, for instance, are not equivalent acts and have widely varying consequences. While they may each evoke similar emotions, absent from the former is a concrete comprehension of the reality of suffering. Mediation can transmit images and information, but only a replication of reality. In replicating, the audience receives a version of the event. As Stanley Cohen remarks:

> The increased international awareness of atrocities and suffering, the spread of new information technologies, and the globalization of the mass media indeed mean that sovereign states (some of them) are being 'watched' as never before. But representing this information is more difficult than ever. There is a profusion of similar images; lines are blurred between fiction and fact (...); 'reality' is always in inverted commas... (Cohen 2001, 187)

If this is the case and the audience confronts imagery of human suffering at an alienated distance from the reality of human suffering, then it becomes clear how the emergence of the spectacle affects the audience from the outset. By presenting a mediated version of reality, "it makes us voyeurs of the suffering of others, tourists amidst their landscapes of anguish" (Ignatieff 1985, 59). The spectacle creates a misapprehension of unity and when this euphoric feeling of solidarity through television attempts to be translated into political action, it produces fickle expressions and capricious reactions.

Instead of witnesses in the traditional sense, the spectacle of suffering produces spectators: Those audiences that watch without engaging, willfully detached from reality. Television proves it is no cure-all. Human rights and humanitarian crises are treated as newsworthy, and even given serious coverage over an extended period of time, but the mediated version beamed into the homes of the viewers maintains moral and geographical distance. "What determines the possibility of being affected morally by photographs is the existence of a relevant political consciousness. Without a politics, photographs of the slaughter-bench of history will likely be experienced as, simply, unreal" (Sontag 1977, 19). There is an acknowledgment of the suffering of others, but the emotional experience does not translate into sustained and meaningful political participation.

Absent political consciousness, an emotional mass outpouring is vulnerable to manipulation. While human rights organizations seek to capitalize on sensational reporting of human rights abuse, power elites and media outlets also wrestle over the message—and the evidence above suggests that these actors, not human rights NGOs, are more competent and savvy in this area:

> We cannot understand, nor have a properly political relation to…atrocities…in the present and future if we do not attend to the centrality of image production and management in them. We will be at an even greater loss if we do not admit that the high-speed electronic news media have created news opportunities not just for activism and awareness, but also for performance, presentation, advertising, propaganda, and for political work of all kinds. (Keenan 2004, 442–43)

Building a broad base of support for transnational advocacy requires not only mastering media tactics, but also cultivating the political consciousness prepared to filter imagery appropriately and direct emotional response for human rights action.

As the spectacle degrades the notion of witness and replaces acting with looking, it transforms another fulcrum on which the movement has always depended. Since the founding of Amnesty International, the "mobilization of shame" has been a reliably useful strategy to defend human rights. Following Somalia, villains in Bosnia and elsewhere not only cease avoiding coverage of their crimes; many begin to deliberately expose themselves and cleverly use imagery to their advantage. If human rights organizations are unable to seize control over narrative and foster solidarity and political consciousness among constituents, then the contested terrain of the visual has been ceded to belligerents and abusers. This dynamic fundamentally turns human rights advocacy on its head, demanding an entirely new approach to the use of information, from documentation to outreach. In an environment in which merely shining light into dark corners is lacking in moral force, NGOs shifted emphasis on mobilizing supporters and galvanizing political will. If only public awareness could be brought to bear, perhaps state power could be pressured into serving the interests of transnational advocacy.

Notes

1. Interview with Susan Osnos, September 22, 2014.
2. Perhaps the most graphic image of Menzel's work from his time in Somalia is of a slaughtered camel bleeding out on the side of the road, having been killed for meat. The photograph is featured in a 1993 article in *Mother Jones* magazine critical of the intervention (Bonner 1993). On the first page of the article, the image is simply of blood running on concrete, while on the second page the blood is revealed to be that of a dead camel, not a dead human. Four pages later, a Save the Children solicitation ad appears before the end of the article featuring two starving children with swollen bellies. NGO appeals intertwined with crisis coverage are common features of the spectacle of suffering.
3. For detailed expositions on the policy debates, see Nicholas Wheeler (2000), Samantha Power (2007), and Jon Western (2005).
4. In her book *Alone Together* (2011), sociologist Sherry Turkle critiques the social impact of digital life, echoing Debord's earlier allusions to "lonely crowds."

References

Amnesty International. 1992. "Somalia: A Human Rights Disaster." AFR 52/01/92. http://www.amnesty.org/en/library/asset/AFR52/001/1992/en/41d08085-ed9b-11dd-9ad7-350fb2522bdb/afr520011992en.pdf.

Baudrillard, Jean. 2008a. "Pornography of War." In *The Jean Baudrillard Reader*, edited by Steve Redhead. New York: Columbia University Press.

———. 2008b. "The Gulf War: Is It Really Taking Place?" In *The Jean Baudrillard Reader*, edited by Steve Redhead. New York: Columbia University Press.

Black, Maggie. 1992. *A Cause for Our Times: Oxfam: The First 50 Years*. Oxford: Oxford University Press.

Bonner, Ray. 1993. "Why We Went." *Mother Jones*, April 1993.

Budabin, Alexandra C., and Joel R. Pruce. 2016. "Beyond Naming and Shaming: New Modalities of Information Politics in Human Rights." *Journal of Human Rights* 15 (3): 408–25.

Bush, George H.W. 1992. "Address on Somalia." December 4. http://millercenter.org/president/speeches/speech-3984.

Castells, Manuel. 2004. "Informationalism, Networks, and the Network Society: A Theoretical Blueprint." In *The Network Society: A Cross-Cultural Perspective*, edited by Manuel Castells. Cheltenham, UK: Edward Elgar Publishing.

Cohen, Stanley. 1996. "Government Responses to Human Rights Reports: Claims, Denials, and Counterclaims." *Human Rights Quarterly* 18 (3): 517–43.

———. 2001. *States of Denial: Knowing About Atrocities and Suffering*. Cambridge: Polity Press.

Cookman, Claude. 2008. "Gilles Caron's Coverage of the Crisis in Biafra." *Visual Communication Quarterly* 15 (4): 226–42.

Dauber, Cori E. 2001. "The Shots Seen Round the World: The Impact of the Images of Mogadishu on American Military Operations." *Rhetoric & Public Affairs* 4 (4): 653–87.

de Montclos, Marc-Antoine Pérouse. 2009. "Humanitarian Aid and the Biafra War: Lessons Not Learned." *Africa Development* 34 (1): 69–82.

de Waal, Alex. 1997. *Famine Crimes: Politics & the Disaster Relief Industry in Africa*. London: African Rights and the International African Institute.

Debord, Guy. 1983. *Society of the Spectacle*. Translated by Ken Knabb. London: Rebel Press.

"Famine Amongst War in Somalia." 1992. *NBC Nightly News*. http://www.youtube.com/watch?v=pRtg65_fj8o.

Friedman, Thomas L. 2005. *The World Is Flat: A Brief History of the Twenty-First Century*, 1st ed. New York: Farrar, Straus and Giroux.

Gotham, Kevin Fox, and Daniel A. Krier. 2008. "From the Culture Industry to the Society of the Spectacle: Critical Theory and the Situationist International." *Current Perspectives in Social Theory* 25: 155–92.

Harrison, Paul, and Robin Palmer. 1986. *News Out of Africa: Biafra to Band Aid*. London: Hilary Shipman Limited.

Heerten, Lasse. 2009. "The Biafran War in Britain: An Odd Alliance of Late 1960s Humanitarian Activists." *Journal of the Oxford University History Society* 7 (Special Issue-Colloquium 2009).

Hochschild, Adam. 1999. *King Leopold's Ghost: A Story of Greed, Terror, and Heroism in Colonial Africa*. Boston: Mariner Books.

Human Rights Watch. 1992. "No Mercy in Mogadishu: The Human Cost of the Conflict and the Struggle for Relief." New York: Human Rights Watch. http://www.hrw.org/legacy/reports/1992/somalia/.

Ignatieff, Michael. 1985. "Is Nothing Sacred? The Ethics of Television." *Daedalus* 114 (4): 57–78.

Iman. 1992. "Somalia Diary." *Vogue* 182 (12): 246.

Keenan, Thomas. 2002. "Publicity and Indifference: Media, Surveillance, 'Humanitarian Intervention'." In *Ctrl [Space] : Rhetorics of Surveillance from Bentham to Big Brother*, edited by Thomas Y. Levin, Ursula Frohne, and Peter Weibel, 544–61. Cambridge, MA: MIT Press.

———. 2004. "Mobilizing Shame." *South Atlantic Quarterly* 103 (2/3): 435–49.

Kellner, Douglas. 2003. *Media Spectacle*. London: Routledge.

Mamdani, Mahmood. 2007. "The Politics of Naming: Genocide, Civil War, Insurgency." *London Review of Books* 29 (5): 8.

Médecins Sans Frontières. 2013. *Somalia 1991–1993: Civil War, Famine Alert and a UN "Military-Humanitarian" Intervention*. http://speakingout.msf.org/en/somalia.

Moeller, Susan D. 1999. *Compassion Fatigue: How the Media Sell Disease, Famine, War and Death*. New York: Routledge.

Mutua, Makau. 2001. "Savages, Victims, and Saviors: The Metaphor of Human Rights." *Harvard International Law Journal* 42 (1): 201–45.

Omaar, Rakiya, and Alex de Waal. 1993. "Disaster Pornography from Somalia." *Media and Values*, no. 61: 13–14.

Power, Samantha. 2007. *"A Problem from Hell": America and the Age of Genocide*. New York: Harper Perennial.

Sliwinski, Sharon. 2011. *Human Rights in Camera*. Chicago: University of Chicago Press.

Sontag, Susan. 1977. *On Photography*. New York: Farrar, Straus and Giroux.

Turkle, Sherry. 2011. *Alone Together: Why We Expect More from Technology and Less from Each Other*, 1st ed. New York: Basic Books.

"U.S. Marines Land in Somalia." 1992. *ABC News*. http://abcnews.go.com/Archives/video/dec-1992-us-marines-land-somalia-15121747.

Western, Jon. 2005. *Selling Intervention and War: The Presidency, the Media, and the American Public*. Baltimore: John Hopkins University Press.

Wheeler, Nicholas J. 2000. *Saving Strangers: Humanitarian Intervention in International Society*. Oxford: Oxford University Press.

Zelizer, Barbie. 1998. *Remembering to Forget: Holocaust Memory through the Camera's Eye*. Chicago: University of Chicago Press.

CHAPTER 5

Bumper Sticker Advocacy and the Branding of Save Darfur

Introduction

Pious supporters may shudder to consider moral defenders of dignity engaged in the work of advertising. Human rights advocates may call it "messaging" or "framing," but these are only palatable pseudonyms for what the corporate sector calls marketing. And they should know. Thorough programs to cultivate image and elevate name recognition are central to the corporate communication efforts that permeate global culture: slogans, logos, spokespersons, and jingles. Branding, in this sense, is the process by which a product is attributed a feeling, an identity, and an association that consumers connect to over time, building loyalty and attachment. If corporate marketing contains effective tools for managing and disseminating strategic information, then perhaps it is precisely the model human rights advocates have always needed. As much as this may cause the human rights core to cringe—as if the self-evident nobility of human rights should operate outside the crude marketplace—if the imperative to raise public awareness is a crucial objective, then why not employ advertising professionals to steer a human rights campaign?

Lessons from Somalia and Bosnia compelled human rights advocates to reflect on how to best leverage and deploy information, in order to mobilize the public and hold officials accountable. An industrious reporter who witnessed the Bosnian genocide firsthand made it her personal mission to reorient the human rights community in this direction: Samantha Power, in her Pulitzer Prize-winning book, *A Problem from*

J. R. Pruce, *The Mass Appeal of Human Rights*, Human Rights Interventions, https://doi.org/10.1007/978-3-319-92075-7_5

Hell: America and the Age of Genocide (2007), a deft chronicle of twentieth-century genocides from the perspective of American policymakers, argues that mass atrocity was permitted to take place over and over again due to a lack of political will within the governments of the great power. Therefore, she concludes, should civil society exact costs from elected officials for their inaction, the necessary will could be generated to halt crimes against humanity in progress or even prevent them from the beginning.

Throughout the book, US Congress members and State Department desk officers attest to this notion with remarks that suggest a degree of democracy in foreign policy that runs contrary to common conception. US Senator Paul Simon stated this clearly when the Rwandan genocide was at a precipice: "If every member of the House and Senate had received 100 letters from people back home…when the crisis was first developing, then I think the response would have been different" (Power 2007, 377). Anthony Lake, National Security Advisor, echoed these sentiments: "If you want to make this move [to send troops and stop massacres], you will have to change public opinion…You must make more noise" (Power 2007, 377). The strength of Power's work is its ability to get behind the façade of "we didn't know about it," when in fact there has been high-level intelligence of each genocide she covers. As a result, her reporting left a legacy among readers with regard to the second step in the equation: Once we know about atrocities, we must "make noise" until we are heard, loud and clear. The final corollary suggests that, if civil society makes enough noise, democratically elected officials will alter their stances and elevate human rights as a foreign policy priority.

This is a forceful sentiment. It empowers citizens to become engaged in human rights advocacy with a specific charge. As well, this lesson compels human rights NGOs to direct their attention and resources to mobilization strategies. If knowing about atrocities is not enough to stop them, then these witnessing audience members must be operationalized through pressure politics. With this driving impetus and the great weight of the Rwandan genocide close in the rear-view mirror, the architects of the movement to end atrocities in Darfur, Sudan, made every attempt to mobilize compassionate citizens and amplify their collective calls for the protection of civilians. Should they succeed in gathering a critical mass of supporters behind the cause, Power's prophecy would be realized and the people of Darfur would in fact be saved. Toward this end, the movement deployed the tools of the twenty-first-century marketing industry in the service of human rights.

From the use of popular culture to the insistence on visual media, the sprawling Save Darfur Campaign demonstrated a capacity to learn from the past while profoundly expanding upon the common tools and tested strategies of human rights organizations. Cultivating consciousness for genocide prevention and fostering a standing community of advocates were cast as specific goals, largely in light of the human rights movement's uneven past. Nostalgia for the breakthrough against Apartheid filtered through the searing memory of inaction in Rwanda culminates in a synthesis that fundamentally informs the approach of the Save Darfur Coalition (SDC).

The movement for Darfur exhibited all the characteristics of a successful human rights initiative: It captured steady news headlines, motivated key policymakers to stake out positions, and mobilized a very broad constituency. Saving Darfur became the subject of bake sales, benefit concerts, opinion pieces, and episodes of television drama, and was thrust into public dialogue with a sense of great urgency. Tens of thousands rallied in the US capitol, and the campaign carried significant celebrity endorsements. The fervor was miraculous in many respects. In a few short years, Darfur was transformed from "a remote Sudanese province little known even to Africanist scholars" (De Waal 2008, 43), into the object of tremendous outrage and compassion, captivating public imagination and generating excitement in high school classrooms, college campuses, and houses of worship. Citizen advocacy captured ideal expressions of cosmopolitan solidarity and the potential for human rights norms to structure a transnational grassroots movement. Darfur was *the* cause célèbre in the decade following 9/11—a repository for the hopes of Western publics aspiring for positive global engagement in the era of the "war on terror" and invasion of Iraq.

Key movement architects, including John Prendergast and George Clooney, describe how profoundly the lessons of Rwanda shaped the founding of Save Darfur. Paramount among those lessons was the necessity to motivate political will through the mobilization of citizens and the articulation of a clear message. Repeatedly referencing Romeo Dallaire's first-hand account (2004) and Samantha Power's journalistic chronicle of the 1994 massacres, the founders of Save Darfur sought to generate sufficient public uproar and go beyond "awareness raising." In Bosnia, Rwanda, and now Darfur, the defense of "we didn't know" was no longer defensible. The crisis in Darfur presented an opportunity for the human rights community to transcend this intuition. The future challenge for mass atrocities prevention would be to operationalize the awareness of abuse and channel outrage into political demands.

In crucial ways, Save Darfur's outreach methods were symptomatic of the time in which they were produced. Shifts in the media landscape coupled with the cultural penetration of corporate branding compelled human rights advocacy to follow suit. Rather than relying on battle-tested techniques that strive for accuracy in storytelling, Save Darfur engaged in a branding campaign that surrendered credibility in exchange for publicity. Save Darfur departed from the Amnesty International/Human Rights Watch model of factual reporting deployed to shame violators. Debates over precisely how many people were dying in Darfur, and why, were largely ignored. Mass appeal was the clear the priority for Save Darfur and in the pursuit of this goal they retained the assistance of subcontracted campaign firms and marketing agencies. The trouble is, however, in advocacy the truthfulness of terminology and certitude of claims matter tremendously. What is lost when moral authority becomes compromised and what does this mean for the future of human rights?

Save Darfur blazed a new path, developing a style all its own by adopting established tactics and injecting them with the full force of Madison Avenue strategies. In its peak year, Save Darfur spent nearly $50 million on its total operations, 60% of which was spent on advertising. The organization relied heavily on independent contractors to complete many of its central functions, such as fund-raising, coordination, and governmental relations. Core leadership worked alongside professional campaign managers and communications directors hired to maximize diffusion of the Save Darfur message. Employing a skeletal top-down management staff, the coalition provoked a grassroots groundswell. The movement to end atrocities in Darfur arises as a popular surge of energy, while also being coaxed by very carefully selected slogans and images. In order for this strategy to be effective, the public must be saturated with clear and concise information about Darfur that cuts through the noisy, fractured media environment. To articulate a platform for the movement, Save Darfur turned to private sector professionals to craft and transmit an image of the coalition that would resonate with the audience.

The branding of Save Darfur hinged on the moral cachet of the genocide label, as the crime of all crimes, and sought to transpose the opposition to "genocide" from a legal interpretation into a fashionable symbol of global citizenship. Appropriating the language for the purpose of recruitment leverages the iconic nature of genocide and relies on its cultural allure to persuade the audience to participate. Affixing the brutal crime to a bumper sticker visibly anchors genocide prevention to the appearance of its supporters and facilitates viral diffusion of the message. The attempt to pre-package the conflict in quick, lucid bites was effective in motivating average people to care about a crisis a world away, but these efforts also produced significant obstacles that not only harmed Save Darfur's stated objectives but also denigrated and cheapened the currency of the crime of genocide.

Once Save Darfur deployed the genocide moniker, the organization stepped out on a ledge from which it could not come down. As circumstances on the ground changed, as the label itself proved divisive, and as the coalition faltered, there could be no rebranding campaign. The coalition sold its masses of supporters on the concept of genocide, so as contradictory evidence emerges and as the nature of the conflict evolves as conflicts do, the narrative remains the same. Eschewing standard practices in favor of self-promotion, the SDC became the focal point of its own campaigns at the expense of the vulnerable civilians it purported to want to "save." The movement suffered from a genuine disconnect: Advertising became a self-perpetuating end in itself, rather than a means to upholding human dignity.

Early Stages of Movement-Building

NGOs Report on Violence in Darfur

Anniversaries have a way of marking time and insisting on reminiscence. Almost exactly ten years after the Rwandan genocide galvanized the global public with horrific tales of raw, violence, another African conflict would bring those memories flooding back and awaken "arguably the largest international social movement since anti-apartheid" (Lanz 2009, 669). Initiated in the USA and remaining largely an American phenomenon, the movement to end atrocities in Darfur, Sudan, reached from elementary school classrooms to Hollywood to the halls of Congress. While the movement emerged spontaneously, its growth was orchestrated by a cadre of foreign policy veterans and well-connected members of the non-profit world through a series of new organizations formed to respond to the crisis: the SDC, the Genocide Intervention Network, and Students Taking Action Now: Darfur! (STAND). Well prior to these fledgling organizations becoming active, established human rights NGOs were already on the case.

As early as February 2003, Amnesty International issued a press release warning of a deteriorating situation in the western region of Darfur and describing attacks on civilians by "armed horsemen" and retaliation against government target, apparently by "bandits" (Amnesty International 2003a). The report described ugly scenes of abduction and random violence against villagers, bodies shot and discarded into fires set by looters who had razed crops and homes (Amnesty International 2003a). While the press release expressed concern about an escalating cycle of violence, as well as grievances by those local bandit groups, it did not demonstrate awareness of the organization of rebels in the area as well as the origins of these horsemen. A month later, UN Human Rights Coordinator for Sudan, Mukesh Kapila, was quoted as saying that Darfur was the site of "the world's greatest humanitarian crisis" and "the only difference between Rwanda and Darfur is now the numbers involved" (Prunier 2007, 127). Despite this ending Kapila's tenure in Sudan, having been transferred by the UN out of country, the comparison to Rwanda—and therefore to genocide—now circulated freely among observers (Crilly 2010, 168).

By April, Amnesty called for Darfur to be folded into the monitoring directives of the peace process governing the North–South Sudanese civil war that had raged since the 1980s, despite being unrelated to the civil war (Amnesty International 2003b). In June, the International Crisis Group (ICG) issued its first report on this splinter conflict and similarly recommended the inclusion of Darfur into to the peacekeeping infrastructure already in place (International Crisis Group 2003). The alarms were sounding of rising rates of violence and human rights abuse against innocents, but, besides Kapila, there were no broader arguments made about the violence. It was not until vocal journalists and commentators became involved that accusations were levied as to the intentional, systematic, and coordinated nature of the attacks.

NGO reporting continued to follow the events unfolding in Darfur throughout 2003. However, much of this news flew under the radar as the public became consumed with the US–UK invasion of Iraq.

Eric Reeves, a US English professor and follower of Sudanese affairs who became a vocal defender of Darfuri rights online and in public debates, first blogged about Darfur on October 8, 2003. The government had begun an aerial assault on the region, in violation of a cease-fire agreement, sending 75,000 refugees fleeing over the border into Chad (Reeves 2003). As these attacks continued, often combining ground forces supported by aerial bombardment, the UN Office for the Coordination of Humanitarian Affairs issued updates through its IRIN news agency of refugee figures and details of the campaign against villages. It would not be until March 24 of the following year that the conflict reached the desk of Nicholas D. Kristof, columnist at the *New York Times* (Kristof 2004).

Kristof was preoccupied for much of 2003 urging against the invasion of Iraq and criticizing the Bush administration's march to war and post-invasion programming, among other pet issues such as human trafficking, preventable disease, and women's rights. In the initial column, the term "ethnic cleansing" was invoked to describe the violence, due to Kristof's framing of the attacks as against "black Africans" and by "lighter-skinned Arab raiders, the Janjaweed" (Kristof 2004). Over the years of the conflict, there were accounts of racial epithets used by the Janjaweed as they maraud through villages, and there are real distinctions to be made between the Islamic elements in northern Sudan that differ from the tribal ethnicities of the people in Darfur that largely affiliate as Masseleit, Fur, and Zaghawa (inter alia Reeves 2003). This description of the conflict was seized upon by observers and activists, including the SDC, and became a conceptual framework for explaining the context for violence in movement literature and talking points. However, the racial dimension also evaded another, seemingly more accurate description of the conflict as one between the government and a rebel faction, in which the government used overwhelmingly brutal tactics against the rebels' civilian base of support. For critics, the racial argument was evidence of deeper ties between the activist organizations and the US government to the extent that the vilifying of Arab violence could be included in the grander narrative of the Bush administration's war on terror (Mamdani 2007).

But, Sudan was not a new issue produced for the benefit of geopolitics. Since the earlier civil war raged, a civil society constituency had been engaged in the east African state, largely to defend the Christian populations in the South from the Muslim regime in the North. Christian

Solidarity International (CSI) is one such group: a self-described human rights organization devoted to the defense of those facing religious persecution, at-risk children, and humanitarian relief (Christian Solidarity International 2017). CSI has been at the forefront of combating modern slavery in Africa by using the controversial method of buying back slaves from slave traders. In June 2004, CSI helped form the Sudan Campaign, along with members of the US Congressional Black Caucus, who "held daily protests in front of the Sudanese embassy [in Washington, DC], allowing themselves to be arrested for obstructing the embassy entrance as an act of civil disobedience" (Hamilton and Hazlett 2007, 341). The movement to Save Darfur is marked by a diverse collaboration, beginning with Evangelical Christians and African–American politicians, soon joined by an influential Jewish group associated with genocide prevention efforts.

A Meeting at a Museum

The Committee of Conscience at the US Holocaust Memorial Museum (USHMM) was established in 1995, two years after the opening of the museum itself, and in 2000 issued its first genocide warning for southern Sudan. Ethnic groups in the south, such as the Dinka and Nuer, were claimed to be under threat from Khartoum, whose actions "are primarily responsible for the deaths of around two million people" and "another four to five million people have been driven from their homes" (Committee of Conscience 2000). On April 7, 2004, the Committee "strongly reiterated" its previous warning, though this time the ethnic groups were different and potential deaths as a consequence of displacement was named as the cause for alarm—highly unconventional evidence of the commission of genocide (Committee of Conscience 2004). Over the subsequent months, the Committee stepped up its calls for attention, received exposure in mainstream media, and pressured elected officials to take stances, as well. By early summer, an umbrella group formed in New York to address the massive violence in Darfur.

An Emergency Summit was convened on July 14, 2004, at the City University of New York at the direction of Jerry Fowler, Staff Director of the Committee of Conscience at the USHMM, and Ruth Messinger of the American Jewish World Service. Representatives from CSI were invited, as were civil rights groups, Muslim charities, human rights organizations, and other relevant civil society actors (Crilly 2010, 170).

Elie Wiesel, renowned Holocaust survivor, Nobel laureate, and anti-genocide activist, provided keynote remarks, and John Prendergast, "who would soon become one of the most ubiquitous Darfur experts" was also on the program (Hamilton and Hazlett 2007, 344). Prendergast served on the National Security Council under President Bill Clinton and has held a range of prominent positions at organizations such as Human Rights Watch and the International Crisis Group. The proceedings produced a Unity Statement declaring violence being perpetrated against civilians in Darfur to be unconscionable and called upon world leaders and international organizations to act. This statement served as the cornerstone of the coalition and larger movement and is an appeal for protest: "We stand together and unite our voices to raise public awareness and mobilize a massive response to the atrocities in Sudan's western region of Darfur" (Save Darfur Coalition 2004). Nearly a week later, the US Congress unanimously passed a resolution declaring the situation in Darfur to be genocide. That same day, July 22, 2004, Secretary of State Colin Powell met with Secretary-General Kofi Annan on Sudan, and both recognized the gravity of what was happening and what could happen, but neither were willing to use the genocide label (Corey 2004). Public pressure rose steadily and resolutely over the subsequent period due entirely to the advocacy of those associated with the SDC.

Over 180 diverse organizations, which may vehemently disagree on a range of other issues, signed on to be a part of SDC and champion the cause. Principal within this broad coalition is the student contingent. On September 14, 2004, ninety Georgetown undergraduate students attended a panel discussion on the crisis in Darfur at USHMM organized by an intern, Lisa Rogoff, from which would emerge STAND. STAND's founders, Ben Bixby, Martha Heinemann, and Nate Wright, set out to end the conflict over the course of fall semester (Hamilton and Hazlett 2007, 345). STAND became the fulcrum of a movement on college campuses around the issue of Darfur that emerged spontaneously but found centralization useful. National days of action could be issued throughout the network that reached from universities to elementary and high schools. Specifically, divestment efforts begun on college campuses by STAND chapters first targeted their own universities' funds for re-appropriation.

A month later, three students at Swarthmore College, Sam Bell, Mark Hanis, and Andrew Sniderman, founded the Genocide Intervention Fund (a name that would be changed to Genocide Intervention

Network, or GI-Net) with the hopes of raising enough money to fund peacekeeping operations in Sudan to protect civilians (Zengerle 2006). To accomplish this bold objective, GI-Net initiated a web-based fund-raising drive and, as the money began flowing in, the fledgling organization needed to find a recipient for an initial sum of $250,000. In due time, they ran through a range of possible options including giving directly to the African Union (AU) or funneling the cash into Rwanda as proxy and then to the AU. These entrepreneurs then began to contact private security firms, with the hope that GI-Net could send contract soldiers into Sudan. After dozens of positive responses, even one unnamed company that agreed to intervene even without consent from the Sudanese government, GI-Net conceded that "going with mercenaries was a bad idea" (Zengerle 2006). Eventually, the money was given to an African NGO partnered with the European Union to "train a contingent of female escorts to protect Darfurian women when they leave their refugee camps to search for firewood" (Zengerle 2006). Genocide Intervention Network raised over $1.6 million and became a formative part of the Save Darfur movement, transitioning from dorm room scheme to Beltway presence (Preston 2006).

The SDC itself served as the hub of the movement around which these other moving parts revolved. Beginning initially with a six-month grant, SDC's leadership believed that a half-year push would be sufficient to mobilize the political will to affect the violence. What can only be described as naïve and short-sighted, SDC, STAND, and GI-Net each exhibited acute inexperience in its outlook and goal-setting. Perhaps a symptom of willful idealism, a senior architect of the SDC remarked to me: "the more I become aware of coalition efforts, the less I come to believe that coalitions have visions." As unusual as this sounds, it speaks to the fluid nature of these early months and years. Having articulated a Unity Statement, SDC personnel were tasked to translate abstract language into policy asks and design a strategy to provide political cover for those prescriptions. The story of the SDC is of a fast-climbing human rights organization that dispensed with the formalities of building infrastructure or articulating strategic vision in exchange for expediency. Responding to an ongoing crisis did not permit a more deliberative or reflective process, in the eyes of executive staff. Gunning at full speed, Save Darfur cut corners in its rise, engaging in a series of trade-offs with significant impact on the trajectory of the movement.

Movement Rising and Striding

Skeleton Crew and Corporate Subcontracts

The SDC began as a small group of activists committed to making the world care about its cause. In that, it succeeded. However, as we investigate the structure of the movement, it becomes clear how non-traditional this whole enterprise was, relative to other major players in the world of transnational human rights advocacy. The core staff met regularly, often daily, to formulate an agenda and discuss operations. Planning occurred against a three-month time horizon, constantly revising and revisiting. There was no five-year strategy. The group strung together funds to match its ambitions and, as it accumulated momentum, both funds and ambition scaled up. As new initiatives emerged, SDC added consultants to conduct key programs. Particularly in the areas of media and communications, outsourced positions cycled in and out regularly. The mainstays that withstood internal dispute and external pressure were those individuals housed outside of Save Darfur proper, those employed by M+R Strategic Services—a firm vital to the rise of the Save Darfur brand.

Seed grants, private giving, and revenues from merchandise underwrote the early years of the movement. Email solicitation proved to be highly effective. Communication strategies were managed by internal directors in consultation with external advisers retained by Save Darfur. Public relations, campaign management, and grassroots mobilization were outsourced through the contracting of independent firms for whom Save Darfur became a client. The organization itself operated with a skeletal, stripped-down staff while much of the work was facilitated through these outside companies. M+R donated shared office space in Washington, DC, to Save Darfur, and individuals working on the account describe a natural, organic, and symbiotic relationship. Rather than patron–client, the Save Darfur project became a labor of love for both employees and contractors for the Coalition.

M+R was on board as early as August 2005 and responsible for "providing communications, online advocacy, fund-raising and advertising, and event planning services" (M+R Strategic Services 2011). With an emphasis on the public interest, M+R's clients are nonprofit organizations, labor unions, and philanthropic foundations, including Oxfam America, Human Rights Campaign, American Diabetes Association,

Service Employees International Union, and the John D. and Catherine T. MacArthur Foundation. The firm projects itself as a synthesis of traditional grassroots activism and cutting edge digital techniques. Boasting its success in capturing media attention and raising the profile of the Save Darfur movement, M+R quantifies awareness raised in terms of email listserv figures, attendance at mass rallies, online postcards sent, and dollars raised. Also associated with New York lobbying firm Malkin and Ross, M+R Strategic Services is a major player in the area of issue-based communication in the USA. The president of M+R, Bill Wasserman, occupied the role of interim executive director of Save Darfur in between the tenures of Rubenstein and Fowler.

As the campaign ramped up, another significant contract was extended to Weber Shandwick, a global public relations firm. Weber Shandwick is an award-winning agency recognized for its prominence and influence in the field. Its client list includes an impressively wide range of corporations including Pepsi, American Airlines, ExxonMobil, Microsoft, KFC, and Johnson & Johnson (Bush 2010). With offices in seventy-seven countries, Weber Shandwick is a subsidiary of the Interpublic Group and in 2013 registered $700 million in fee income (Sudhaman 2014). Weber's brand communication emphasizes new attempts to humanize corporations in the eyes of consumers through efforts in social responsibility, corporate citizenship, and environmental consciousness. The agency takes on public affairs and government clients as well, which include UN Woman's HeForShe gender equity campaign and the Obama administration's efforts to publicize enrollment procedures for the Affordable Care Act.

Save Darfur's single highest expense, as well as the greatest proportion of the budget, occurred at GMMB, a "political consulting and advocacy advertising firm." In 2007 alone, SDC spent $32,982,042 on its contract with GMMB, or over 64% of its total expenses for that year. The agency runs campaigns for organizations on malaria prevention, youth tobacco use, methamphetamine abuse, and cancer awareness. In the electoral arena, GMMB's clients include prominent Democratic members of Congress, such as Senators Barbara Boxer and Harry Reid, President Bill Clinton, South African President Nelson Mandela, and President Barack Obama. Personnel moved fluidly from the campaign team and the administration, into GMMB since 2008 (post-dating its involvement with Save Darfur). A full-service agency, GMMB oversees all processes of its campaigns, from grassroots organizing and strategy development, to digital marketing and video production. GMMB is owned by its parent company Omnicom Group, and its stock is held by Fleishman-Hillard, another global behemoth of advertising. Along with sizeable investments in strategic consulting and other areas of public relations, Save Darfur was in business with high-profile firms from the corporate world and major movers in the domestic political arena.

The intersection of advocacy and advertising should not surprise us, however. The profound penetration of corporate culture in and through global society breeds one-dimensional public engagement: Corporations assume an "ethical" posture while molding a political sector in its own image. I insist that as these distinctions blur, the adversarial nature of political advocacy and the antagonistic content of its claims collapses. The aesthetics and messaging get processed through the corporate form generating logos and slogans that are prefabricated and "predigested," to use Adorno's language. Human rights campaigns bear the look and feel of corporate marketing, and while agencies like Weber Shandwick are adept at advertising products, now the products are human rights demands rather than consumer goods. In quite literal terms, human rights claims are commodified as they are packaged and branded for mass appeal, which prompts a critical question motivating this chapter and the book: What is the impact of the commodified form on the content of human rights advocacy?

Targets and Tactics

As Save Darfur began its outreach efforts, strategy focused on grabbing headlines and galvanizing broad public support. In early 2005, Nick Kristof received a cache of photographs from Brian Steidle, a US Marine stationed as an observer with the African Union. Steidle traveled places journalists could not and captured images of barbarity that the Western audiences had not yet seen: dead bodies strewn on a sandy landscape and villages razed to ash. Kristof managed to publish four color photographs in his February 23 column, a highly uncommon feature in the *New York Times* opinion page. Steidle was a strong voice and outspoken advocate. He traveled across the country and visited twenty-one cities on a speaking tour sponsored by Save Darfur, called "Million Voices for Darfur." In addition to these events, Steidle wrote a memoir and produced a widely viewed documentary of his experience in Darfur entitled, *The Devil Came on Horseback*. In tandem, Kristof and Steidle are responsible for a significant portion of the mass diffusion of Darfur information and outrage.

The speaking tour was a highly coordinated program facilitated by Save Darfur communication strategists, hired specifically for this purpose, which neatly exemplifies the top-down/bottom-up strategy. Steidle made stops at colleges and churches, showing his photographs and sharing his stories. The stops were planned in conjunction with local activists in each city, with special attention paid to the elected officials representing that area. As the event neared, Save Darfur worked to place editorials both in local papers and in papers in the nearest the big city. For instance, when Steidle was scheduled to speak in Fort Wayne, Indiana, op-eds would run in newspapers between the smaller city and the state capitol, Indianapolis. Articles were intended to drive readers to the event, raise general awareness for Darfur, as well as attract the attention of Richard Lugar, Indiana Republican Senator and chairman of the Senate Committee on Foreign Relations. This strategic blend of bottom-up and top-down strategy effectively stimulated local activity, which produced postcards and petition signatures, but was much performance as it was practice. For Save Darfur, its grassroots base was never utilized in any direct fashion. The swell of support for the cause coming from places like Fort Wayne, Indiana, was never intended to apply direct pressure on Senator Luger, but instead was meant to represent a mobilized public. This is to say, it was more important to communicate the perception of grassroots activism than it was to operationalize grassroots activism. Standing in, masses of Save Darfur supporters constituted an anonymous crowd to leverage in consultation with decision makers.

In 2006, Save Darfur bought its first print advertisement, placed in the Waco Tribune-Herald in Waco, Texas, the largest paper close to President Bush's Crawford, Texas ranch. In order to raise money for the ad, an email was distributed asking for a minimum $50 donation in exchange for the inclusion of your name on a letter to the president. The email was sent to those who had already signed a pledge as part of the Million Voices for Darfur campaign. When the ad ran, Save Darfur sent a delegation of twenty Sudanese refugees marching to the security gates at Bush's ranch to deliver a symbolic postcard. Attempting to "keep the Darfur genocide on his mind even while he's on vacation," the action was a staged event for local and national media audiences, rather than intended to actually pressure Bush in any meaningful way. These kinds of high-profile displays are in effect one-off gestures to grab the attention of a viewing public and cultivate a general sensibility among them about responsibility and culpability. In only a thin sense is President Bush the actual target of this action. The SDC relies on the spectacle of the event to exert moral pressure on the audience watching the event takes place.

These sorts of stunts continued even as the movement morphed to focus on the world of finance. Save Darfur, GI-Net, and STAND orchestrated a high-profile divestment push to apply pressure against Sudan through firms and companies that profited from their investment in the country's industry. China and PetroChina became a central target, as did Fidelity Investment and Berkshire Hathaway. China's booming economy produced an excessive demand for oil, and Sudanese reserves proved to be indispensable. Therefore, divestment activism highlighted the way in which Western firms held stock in companies that propped up the regime in Khartoum and were complicit in the tremendous violence against civilians in Darfur. Withdraw investment in PetroChina, squeeze Sudan and China economically, and exact retribution for atrocities.

At the metro stop in Boston, beneath the streets that housed the headquarters of Fidelity, Save Darfur plastered posters connecting support for genocide with investment: "Are your riches filthy?" "Are your savings taking life?" "Tell your mutual fund company: Genocide is a bad investment." Messaging was flanked by pictures of refugees in makeshift structures, and children with protruding ribs; the spectacle of suffering was alive and well among the Save Darfur set. The Coalition bought out all the advertising space at this stop and distributed leaflets outside of headquarters for two weeks, "every morning and every lunchtime, in front of the headquarters, so that every staff person at Fidelity was handed a leaflet when they went to work."[1] Save Darfur hired a mobile billboard to drive around the CEO's house. A camera crew was sent to Chad to film an English-speaking Darfuri refugee reading a letter from the head of investor relations claiming that investment decisions are made based on sound financial rationale. The commercial met with tremendous resistance and Fidelity actively intervened to persuade CNN not to run the ad spot; same occurred at Newsweek regarding a corollary print ad. Fidelity claimed that the information contained in the commercial relied on outdated data and was inaccurate. *The New York Times* and the *Boston Globe*, both owned by the same parent company, rejected the ad as well, stating that it unfairly "singles out one company for the actions of many that invest in China's resources" (quoted in Vennochi 2007). Rallies were staged in Boston around the time of this controversy to further amplify public outrage and forcefully argue for the connection between investment and acquiescence to genocide. Berkshire Hathaway received similar treatment, as Save Darfur purchased all the outdoor ad space during its investor conference in Omaha and sent Darfuri refugees to hand out leaflets to all attendees.

This overall strategy was intended to construct a reality around the executives and shareholders at Fidelity and Berkshire that the Darfur issue was popular and that investment with PetroChina was unpopular. Subway advertising was not present in every metro stop in Boston or in every city across the country, but if you get off the train during your morning commute and see these images and quotes constantly, you are given the impression that everyone is seeing the same pictures you are. Similar to the invisible community created through television viewership, advertising has the impact of inventing, implanting, and nurturing shared experiences. Creating this illusion for decision makers at Fidelity was entirely deliberate, intended to be a heavy-handed supplement to broader outreach initiatives targeted at the mass audience. Even the skirmish over the commercial turned into a positive for Save Darfur because it became a newsworthy story, even if the ad never ran. It was all about chasing headlines and media coverage in order to build a bubble of pressure around key players. Again, the actual movement, the grassroots, becomes a backdrop at best here. The communication strategies rely on the moral force of the appearance of outrage, rather than any direct impact of public protest. The audience remains an audience, passive, never fully actualized as a movement of individuals committed to a cause. In tandem with the elite targeting through the tactics described here, mass mobilization hinged on the currency of popular culture, consumerism, and celebrities.

A Merchandising Bonanza and Celebrity Feeding Frenzy

In September 2004, the film *Hotel Rwanda* was released to wide acclaim and direct ties were made between Rwanda and Darfur among the audience. Don Cheadle, who portrayed the hero Paul Rusesabagina, became active in the movement and proved to be an instrumental figure. In reality, Rwanda and Darfur did not share many similarities, except that they are both massively violent conflicts in East Africa. However, the reminder of the 1994 genocide penetrated the 2004 movement and generated "the biggest boost to American popular interest" (Flint and

De Waal 2008, 184). Even in light of this popularity, the audience has a short attention span and the December 26 Asian Tsunami quickly eclipsed Darfur as the cause of the moment. Donations streamed in and news coverage swept up the audience. The tsunami was treated as wholly apolitical and rested on the emotional effect of the devastation, which was severe (Prunier 2007, 128). Coverage of the tsunami dealt a minor media setback to SDC, but one it would overcome. Kristof and Steidle, and the impact from their reportage, catapulted Darfur back into the fore. To deepen the cultural penetration of the issue and raise essential funds, coalition members turned to predictable patterns of consumerism and mass appeal.

Lisa Rogoff, a founder of STAND while working at USHMM, suggested a green, rubber wristband for Darfur, after Lance Armstrong's Livestrong cancer support foundation whose yellow band "had acquired that intangible quality of 'cool' due to the parade of Hollywood stars seen wearing them" (Hamilton and Hazlett 2007, 347). Amnesty International issued a compilation album called "Instant Karma," on which pop stars recorded cover songs written by John Lennon, proceeds from which went to AI's Campaign to Save Darfur. The television medical drama "ER" filmed an episode in South Africa where they staged the scene of a Darfuri refugee camp. "T-shirts, mugs and even underpants emblazoned with messages such as 'Think, Act, Save Darfur' or 'Empower Darfur' could be bought for a few dollars on the internet. The discerning pet could eat dinner from a bowl proclaiming, 'If we don't speak up we become accomplices'" (Crilly 2010, 165).

Students at the University of Southern California even devised a video game called "Darfur is Dying" that allowed the player to occupy the role of a refugee seeking water and evading Janjaweed pursuit (Vargas 2006). Timberland, the footwear and apparel company, partnered with actor and activist Don Cheadle to design a work boot with a message in its tread, "Stomp Out Genocide." Only one hundred pairs of the boots were manufactured and "delivered to humanitarian activists, policy makers, journalists, and entertainment professionals who raised awareness of and championed change in Darfur" (Cheadle and Prendergast 2007, 148–49). Profits from these ventures benefited the budgets of advocacy organizations, provided revenue for operating expenses, and enlisted consumers as viral billboards.

Cheadle, among the most visible celebrities on Darfur, teamed up with John Prendergast for multiple trips to the region, interviews, op-eds, and two books, but he was not alone. Cheadle and Prendergast established the Not On Our Watch foundation and assembled a masthead that veritably mirrored the closing credits of the heist films *Oceans Eleven*, *Twelve*, and *Thirteen*: George Clooney, Brad Pitt, Matt Damon, and Jerry Weintraub. Around the same time, in 2006, Pitt and Angelina Jolie publically announced a $1 million private gift to several Sudanese NGOs (Mamdani 2009, 53).

George Clooney raised the profile of Save Darfur as he raised his profile within the movement. Prior to this involvement, Clooney contacted Bono interested in finding a human rights issue to which to devote his time, remarking that he was interested in Africa. Bono, the prototypical celebrity humanitarian already deeply involved in HIV/AIDS and debt relief, suggested Clooney explore Darfur as an issue that was ramping up and one he could impact. Save Darfur allied itself with Clooney once he approached them, and he is considered to have been a crucial partner: humble, dedicated, and genuine. Clooney sought counsel from his father, a Cincinnati journalist with whom he traveled to Chad and Sudan, notably twice contracting malaria and once bringing along Oprah Winfrey's film crew (Hamilton and Hazlett 2007, 360). Staff members within Save Darfur recall Clooney not requiring scripts or prompting, conducting his own research. SDC orchestrated his trips to the region and coordinated media opportunities but relied on his independence as well. More so than others, Clooney also testified in front of US Congress and for UN committees on Darfur offering impassioned pleas for intervention and civilian protection.

Besides the prominent *Oceans* crowd, Mia Farrow stood out as one who "has dirtied herself in the dust of Darfur" (Crilly 2010, 172). As the 2008 Beijing Olympics approached, Farrow ramped up public attention on the relationship between China and the regime in Khartoum, labeling the global event as the Genocide Olympics. Farrow went on hunger strikes and famously dissuaded film icon Steven Spielberg from directing the opening ceremonies of the Olympics, despite his contract to do so. Leveraging the China issue allowed for spin-offs to materialize, including US speed skater and Wheaties cereal box superstar Joey Cheek's Team Darfur—a coalition of athletes dedicated to the cause of Darfur. Farrow provided the divestment wing of the movement with the greatest exposure and contributed to its many successes including against Fidelity Investments, who would eventually divest over $1 billion from PetroChina. Oddly, Farrow even "approached the private security company Blackwater to see if they were ready to go to Darfur" (De Waal 2008, 44) at a lunch with CEO Erik Prince, signaling yet another episode in a thread of flirtation with militarism that ran just beneath the surface of the movement, at times bubbling up into view.

Celebrities played central roles in Save Darfur: spokespersons, performers, fundraisers, and donors. The most out-front individuals came of their own accord and spoke in their own voices. The coalition coordinated trips to the region, media appearances, and policy asks, but did not provide scripts. Clooney and Farrow were particularly knowledgeable, articulate, and passionate on their own, and useful as recruiters of other famous people to the cause. Spreading across sectors, from film and sports to celebrity politicians, the movement benefited from its association with figures that virtually carry their own camera crews in tow. In an age of paparazzi, wherein every mundane act of celebrities is newsworthy, the coalition was able to rely on their spokespersons to attract coverage of every appearance and event; this relationship permitted Save Darfur to bound over traditional hurdles that human rights issues face in trying to gain traction in public. O.A.R., an American rock band and performer at a 2006 SDC rally, unironically proclaimed its gratitude for being involved in such a worthwhile cause: "it's literally the least we could do" (Save Darfur Coalition 2006). True enough.

Translating Attention into Action

This outpouring of energy and wide-ranging efforts culminated in various mass expressions. On April 30, 2006, the SDC held its biggest national event to date, with a rally in Washington, DC, on the National Mall. Headlining the event were figures such as George Clooney (who only signed on one week earlier), Elie Wiesel, Samantha Power, Paul Rusesabagina, Joey Cheek, and then-Senator Barack Obama. Country music stars Big & Rich performed. With the White House as backdrop, this event decidedly focused on the American response to the atrocities, and the capacity of the public to motivate an official response of some sort. The event represented the culmination of two years of progress on the issue, marked largely by the impressive attendance and the significant media attention it garnered.

In the crowd were cross-sections of the population from Jewish and Armenian groups bused in from throughout the country, to repatriated African refugees. There was criticism about the lack of diversity of speakers (Eichler-Levine and Hicks 2007), but the audience personified the broad base of support that the campaign had cultivated (in the USA). Leading up to the rally, which also consisted of a west coast satellite event in San Francisco, Save Darfur launched a new campaign determined to send one million postcards to President Bush to express public demand to further US commitment. Coalition members, including Amnesty International, participated by using the same text that SDC crafted, but distributing it to their own audience on their own printed materials. Along with a corresponding drive online, in the first quarter of 2006, the email listserv of Save Darfur jumped by 800% (Hamilton and Hazlett 2007, 357). In the fall, another rally was held in Central Park, New York City, as well as at sites throughout the world—a sign that the movement was aware of its limitations as an American movement and the imperative of internationalization (Save Darfur Coalition 2011).

Simultaneously, George Clooney gave testimony to the UN Security Council to supplement the AU force in Darfur which was set to expire at the end of the month: "So after September 30th, you won't need the UN. You will simply need men with shovels and bleached white linen and headstones" (quoted in Mamdani 2009, 54). Clooney in essence had declared the 2007 campaign theme which shifted from attaining critical mass to a sense of impending doom and urgency, the hourglass serving as a de facto mascot. The next year witnessed a wider barrage of mass events. In the spring, a "Global Day for Darfur" was held in forty-seven American states and forty-one countries (Thomas-Jensen and Spiegel 2008, 210–11). "More than 3000 campaigners gathered in London outside Downing Street where a giant hourglass was filled with red liquid to represent the blood spilled so far in the conflict" (Crilly 2010, 163). Film stars Matt Damon and Hugh Grant were photographed for posters in which they aggressively smash blood-filled hourglasses (*BBC* 2007). Mia Farrow hosted a rally in Washington, and activists in Boston participated in a "die-in," in solidarity with those civilians under fire. "All around the world protestors turned hourglasses upside down to demonstrate how time for a solution to be found was running out" (Crilly 2010, 163). Yet, as the movement painted a picture of Darfur as increasingly desperate, the Coalition was about to receive a burst of support it had not anticipated. But as the movement for genocide prevention in Darfur accelerated, its internal tensions produced catastrophic stumbling blocks.

Movement Surges and Stumbles

Following these spectacular events, a donor or set of donors contacted Save Darfur through an intermediary whom the leadership in SDC and M+R trusted, offering a preliminary donation earmarked for advertising purposes. Impressed by the movement's momentum, the donors made payments in a series of installments that would amount to nearly $50 million, although the Coalition was not aware of the full amount initially. The donors believed that in order to propel the movement to the next level, an advertising push would be essential and this suggestion did not clash with the goals and strategies of Save Darfur. As a dose of "healthy jet fuel for this campaign," this influx of cash was spent as quickly as it came in on ad buys across multimedia platforms.[2] Save Darfur was able to negotiate directing some portion of the funds to improving its global presence through advertising in in-flight magazines on planes with destinations in China and elsewhere, and creating the Globe for Darfur—a coalition intended to internationalize the SDC model.[3]

The considerable flood of donor money in Fiscal Year 2007 (October 1, 2006–September 30, 2007) presented an incredible opportunity for Save Darfur, allowing the organization to spend six times what it had the previous year, well in excess of budget projections.[4] While the products of the advertising campaign that followed from the 2006 rallies continued to raise the status of the movement, it also was accompanied by heightened scrutiny of its activities from both allies and natural enemies. Because while the injection of money provided a taller stage and a louder megaphone, it also magnified the movement's own inconsistencies: Save Darfur's reliance on advertising and branding as central devices for outreach and mobilization created distance between the movement and the facts. In its desire to resonate with the audience and motivate political will, affixing the "genocide" label to the conflict became indispensable even as doubts were raised about its truthfulness. If, as this analysis suggests, the SDC consciously or unconsciously chose the branding imperatives of "genocide" over the moral authority of accuracy in reporting, this would mark a severe departure from a foundational cornerstone of human rights advocacy.

Wrestling with the G-Word

Since late 2004, official reports and media outlets trafficked in death figures as high as 500,000 and as low as 35,000 seeking to accurately portray the level of suffering in Darfur. Casualty counts, however, must be disaggregated in a complex humanitarian emergency such as this. Some proportion of the dead will have died directly from violent attacks, and others are accounted for as "excess deaths," those that die from indirect consequences of war: the danger inherent in refugee flight, malnutrition and starvation, unsanitary conditions, disease, and lack of access to medical care, for instance. While these are by no means inconsequential effects of war, excess deaths provide shaky ground on which to advance an argument that the crime under investigation is a genocide.

By spring 2005, several organizations had conducted their own mortality studies that produced divergent results. World Health Organization (WHO) tallied 45,000–80,000 total deaths, with between 35,000 and 70,000 excess deaths. The Center for Research on the Epidemiology of Disasters (CRED), affiliated with WHO, determined excess death to have reached 118,412. US State Department's numbers ranged from 63,000 to 146,000. The Coalition for International Justice (CIJ), a now-defunct NGO partnership financed by the State Department to supplement its own internal investigation, claimed 396,563 total casualties. Eric Reeves maintained a running count on his Web site that reached 400,000 by the end of 2004 and fluctuated from as low as 300,000 up to 500,000 over the course of the next two years (these figures included within a broader discussion at Mamdani 2009, 26–28). In April 2005, SDC began using the 400,000 figure, "a claim based on its previous research and an analysis of other data" (Foley 2008, 9).

The National Academy of Sciences and the Government Accountability Office (GAO), a respected nonpartisan body connected to the US government tasked with auditing various aspects of public life, undertook an expansive study to make sense of this muddle of statistics. Its 2006 report culminated in a thorough analysis of methods and findings of six sources and issued a broad condemnation: "*The experts we consulted did not consistently rate any of the death estimates as having a high level of accuracy*" (emphasis added; US Government Accountability Office 2006, 8). The report consists of quantitative and qualitative assessment of the numbers. The GAO's challenges included controlling for time because studies were conducted in different phases of the conflict and the way in which extrapolation was used by each provided further complication. GAO's critique rested on their inability to compare different states within western Sudan or to properly account for death rates over time. As well, limits in existing population figures, lack of access to the affected areas, and the challenging conditions of collecting data in a conflict zone contributed to a host of problems.

Some of the studies, including that of Reeves, were challenged for lack of objectivity, because they "were more characteristic of advocacy or journalistic material than of objective analysis" (US Government Accountability Office 2006, 32). "Overall, the experts rated CRED's estimates most highly in terms of data, methods, objectivity, and reporting of limitations" (US Government Accountability Office 2006, 21). This placed the number of fatalities at 170,237 in the period September 2003–January 2005, which includes baseline mortality, refugee populations, and 141,800 excess deaths, yielding approximately 35,000 "violence-related deaths" (US Government Accountability Office 2006, 20; Guha-Sapir and Degomme 2005, 35). It is important to keep in mind, however, that the CRED report concludes that excess deaths "may be attributed directly as a consequence of the war" (Guha-Sapir and Degomme 2005, 35). Still, whether these assessments describe a genocide remains a dubious claim.

This conclusion is satisfying and unsatisfying. It presents, on the one hand, a reasonable approximation of deaths in Darfur during the peak period of violence (since the beginning of rebel uprising in February 2003, it would make sense to assume that CRED's figures could be revised slightly higher). As well, the GAO report allows for a juxtaposition of the various numbers that had been widely used in the media and in movement advertising. Yet, it does not solve the dilemma of whether or not genocide was either in progress or had occurred—nor was this its task. The report does not address the question of culpability, nor does it provide specific remarks on intentionality: Excess deaths may be a direct consequence of the war, but does this then compel the conclusion that they were part of a campaign "with intent to destroy, in whole or in part, a national, ethnical, racial or religious group," as the Convention demands?

The nuanced legal and political nature of these questions was not deeply considered by the leadership within Save Darfur. The advocacy imperatives trumped any serious analysis of the language of genocide, aside from its powerful moral currency. Movement architects insist that categorizing the violence as genocide was indispensable to their effort. As well, they believed in the credibility of their information, including the first-hand perspectives of people like Mukesh Kapila. They believed in the inspirational strength of the term, particularly for American Jews, who were at the core of the movement from its inception at the Holocaust Museum. The individuals that shaped and steered Save Darfur have mixed memories about the role played by the genocide label. Some maintain it was essential, while others don't recall leading with it per se. There were no internal debates about the use of the word. Once it was selected, it stayed, even as it increasingly was accompanied by controversy.

My sense is that the Coalition willingly balanced the demand to be accurate with the desire to be resonant—and these two were presumed to be mutually incompatible. While Save Darfur's website was intended to be a source of reliable information, there were omissions that served the interests of the organization, including any reference to atrocities by the rebels in their war against the government, for instance. I was anecdotally told of an unnamed staff member at Human Rights Watch who pushed back against Save Darfur's assertions about the death toll. When asked to provide better information, the Human Rights Watch representative never responded. A complex humanitarian emergency such as Darfur was precisely that, complex. Yet, complexity does not play well through the advertising tactics of a movement striving for mass appeal. To add a final layer of convolution, in the midst of this debate over genocide, the violence in Darfur was actually on the decline. It remained an open question of how to designate the conflict 2003–2006, but by time the donors came forward all numbers were falling. Yet, again, this reality failed to register in the messaging of Save Darfur.

The Persistence of the Genocide Controversy

Journalists and observers initiated the debate as early as 2003–2004, with Mukesh Kapila and Nick Kristof leading the charge. As noted above, the USHMM's Committee on Conscience issued a genocide alert in July, the same month the US Congress passed a resolution declaring the conflict in Darfur to be genocide. Save Darfur's Unity Statement describes Janjaweed violence: "They wiped out entire villages, destroyed food and water supplies, stole livestock and systematically murdered, tortured and raped civilians" (Save Darfur Coalition 2004). Categorizing these paramilitary actions under a centralized directive, SDC connects the dots to formulate an argument: "The Sudanese government's genocidal, scorched earth campaign has claimed hundreds of thousands of lives through direct violence, disease and starvation…" (Save Darfur Coalition 2004). On September 9, President Bush issued a statement and Secretary of State Powell spoke before the Senate Foreign Relations Committee, both of whom declared that genocide was underway, under the direction of the regime in Khartoum (Straus 2005, 130). For the first time, seated high-ranking US officials used the "G-word" to describe an ongoing conflict, triggering the political and moral imperatives of the Genocide Convention. For advocates, this represented "an unimaginable coup" and served to further energize the movement (Hamilton and Hazlett 2007, 343).

Yet, the Bush administration and the SDC were alone. President Bush was a problematic partner particularly by 2004, a year into the invasion of Iraq, making this designation six months after the Abu Ghraib torture revelations. The Bush administration could not lead on human rights, and there is no indication of any intention to match rhetoric with action. Other Western authorities "avoided the term, as did UN Secretary-General Kofi Annan, who was pilloried in the media for limiting his description of Darfur to 'massive violations of human rights'" (Straus 2005, 130). This was indeed the conclusion of the 2005 UN Commission of Inquiry headed by international jurist Antonio Cassese, but surely Annan's interests were also served by evading the genocide language. His intransigence on the issue is evidenced further by his failure to follow-through on Security Council resolutions authorizing a robust peacekeeping mission. A high-ranking leader within Save Darfur, angered by Annan's inertia, forecasts that there will be "a special place in hell for Kofi Annan."[5] But even Samantha Power, the muse of the student movement, preferred the term "ethnic cleansing" for its generality and the uncertainty that the whole group was the target of the violence, rather than the space itself (Straus 2005, 130). None of the most respected human rights NGOs—neither Médecins Sans Frontières (MSF), Amnesty International, nor Human Rights Watch—labeled the crisis in Darfur genocide (Crilly 2010, 181; Fake and Funk 2009, 16). When Bashir is indicted by the International Criminal Court for the crime of genocide in 2010, HRW issues a press release that supports the pursuit of criminal justice for Bashir, but states that it "has not taken a position on whether the crimes constitute genocide due to insufficient information in its research" (Human Rights Watch 2010). The advocacy community was engaged on Sudan but did not stand lockstep with Save Darfur and George W. Bush.

By any metric, Darfur was, at least, unlike other genocides we have seen. It has been described as "a slow-motion genocide" and "genocide by attrition" (Cheadle and Prendergast 2007, 3; Quoting Mia Farrow in Crilly 2010, 180). But, does this match our conception of genocide? Clearly, it is not Rwanda, where 800,000 members of one ethnic group were executed by members of a rival faction in one hundred days, at the command of a central authority that enumerated a detailed list of targets for assassination. Neither is it the Nazi Holocaust or the Serbian campaign against Bosnians, both of which shook the world with its mechanization and systematic efficiency. In the view of one journalist: "Genocides do not wind down after a couple of years, as the slaughter had in Darfur. They end with the victory of one side or the other, when all the victims are dead or the perpetrators are defeated. *There is no such thing as half a genocide*" (emphasis added; Crilly 2010, 182–83). This sentiment is a reflection based on the facts on the ground, as well as based on a certain conception, legal and historical, of what genocide looks like. Depending on how we assess these distinctions, we must either expand the Convention's definition to include new cases and examples, or stick with the original and deny that many instances of mass violence are genocidal.

Rebecca Hamilton distinguishes between an "essentialist" and an "instrumentalist" typology of genocide in which the former corresponds to the most typical cases, such as the Holocaust and Rwanda, while the latter include less obvious choices like South Sudan and Guatemala (2011, 72). Both of these "instrumentalist" instances include large-scale violence and terror against civilians of a particular group but are less frequently included with the classic cases. A key element to this distinction is the question of intent: Was the intent to eliminate the group from the face of the earth, or were the atrocities a means to another end? For instance, if 200,000 civilians are killed or disappeared in the course of a civil war, but the objective of the aggressor was to win the war at any cost, is this a case of genocide? Finally, the essentialist view carries with it an embedded narrative of guilt and innocence that the details of a civil war complicate.

In any event, the controversy created space for supporters of Khartoum to maneuver. "It would be more difficult for the Sudanese government to sidestep accusations of murder. Accusations of genocide allowed it all sorts of ways to get off the hook" (Crilly 2010, 182–83). Naïve to the unintended consequences of its campaigning, Save Darfur continued to ratchet up the pressure with its public relations machine. After all, even in light of new information, how would the Coalition back out of the corner it painted itself into. How do you undo the accusation of genocide? There would be no midstream adjustments or adaptations, even if it might strengthen the advocacy prospects. Genocide might be the vernacular to move an audience morally, but it also presents an exceedingly high proof threshold that al-Bashir gladly circumnavigated by using the UN's own findings against the international community.

Save Darfur was committed to the conclusion that genocide occurred by edict of Khartoum and that justice would be served only when the regime stood to account for its crimes. The scope of the violence and the stories of fleeing refugees of horrific barbarity against civilians moved those people in the early meetings at the Committee of Conscience. They made a gamble on the use of the word genocide and stuck with it to the end and believed in the wisdom of doing so. However, a glaring lesson to be learned and applied for the future is the damaging way in which Save Darfur's messaging got square in the way of its own potential for success. After all, marketing is a means to an end—selling product—not an end unto itself.

Adversity from Without and from Within

In 2007, Executive Director David Rubinstein launched an unprecedented human rights advertising campaign in the USA, as well as in the UK with SDC's British partner, Aegis Trust. Plastering subway cars and billboards with images of a nameless dark-skinned child, with wide, hopeful eyes, in the arms of a woman draped in a vivid orange cloth, Darfur was forced into the public eye. Print ads and television commercials provided a prominent media presence for the grassroots movement. However, despite the GAO's findings, the figure of 400,000 dead remained ubiquitous. This startling number was ruled to be inaccurate yet continued as the official total. Standard text on the printed advertisements read as follows:

> The genocide in Darfur is worsening. Thousands more will die if we don't act. In 2003, Sudanese President Omar al-Bashir moved to crush

> opposition by unleashing vicious armed militates to slaughter entire villages of his own citizens. After three years, 400,000 men, women and children have been killed. 2.5 million driven from their homes. Untold thousands raped, tortured, and terrorized. The efforts of President Bush and other world leaders haven't stopped the horror. President Bashir continues to expand his campaign of terror, killing more innocent people every day.

While inconsistencies may regularly go unnoticed in advertising, a pro-Khartoum constituency was ready and willing to exploit the inflated statistic. The European-Sudanese Public Affairs Council (ESPAC), "an organization funded by Khartoum to defend its interests abroad," filed a claim in the UK against Aegis Trust and SDC with the British Advertising Standards Authority (ASA) (Crilly 2010, 175). ESPAC challenged the merit of the figure and disputed the presentation of this number as fact. David Hoile, the Director of ESPAC, had self-published several monographs discrediting the anti-genocide movement and shifting attention to the role of the rebel groups in Darfur.[6] ASA evaluated the challenge, based on the GAO report and on letters submitted from researcher Dr. John Hagan, the Northwestern University sociologist responsible for the figure of 400,000 as reported originally by the Coalition for International Justice. Conclusively, the ASA decided that SDC's claims were in violation of standards of advertising and must, theretofore, qualify their figures as opinion, rather than as matters of fact. While failing to register in the American media and carrying no legal implications, pressure from this embarrassment complicated matters for Save Darfur (Foley 2008, 9).

This advertising push placed SDC at odds with their opponents, as well as with their friends. By this time, the humanitarian relief effort in Darfur was the largest aid operation on the planet, due in large part to the advocacy of the Save Darfur movement. The attention heaped on Darfur over these years contributed, not only to a heightened sense of political clamoring, but also to a boost in charitable donations. However, in 2007, as this media blitz reached critical mass, a backlash within the community caused tensions to rise. Vocal representatives from prominent aid agencies took issue with Save Darfur on at least two fronts: first, the issue of the death tolls and the cause of death; second, the force-forward message in the advertising. Not only were the misleading figures embarrassing to those working on the ground, including to the extent it provided comfort to the Bashir government, but the campaign projected an image of a conflict fraught with violence. Instead, as relief workers witnessed, the leading killer in 2005–2007 was "diarrheal diseases and malaria," not guns or machetes (Flint and De Waal 2008, 186). Which is why SDC's call for a no-fly zone over Darfur was so illogical from the perspective of humanitarianism: the same measures that would prevent military planes from flying, would also prevent aid drops from continuing, threatening the viability of the operations underway; let alone the danger of collateral damage and the cascading impact of the military effort to enforce a no-fly zone. Furthermore, relief organizations worried that increasing the military presence in Darfur, as SDC proposed through its calls for a multilateral peacekeeping force, could also have unintended consequences for peace and stability.

This tension was exposed in public in 2007 in a series of letters and press statements. Sam Worthington, of InterAction, wrote to SDC in strong terms: "I am deeply concerned by the inability of Save Darfur to be informed by the realities on the ground and to understand the consequences of your proposed actions" (Mamdani 2009, 50). Not only did InterAction take issue with the content of the advocacy, but also the way in which SDC purports to speak for the greater human rights and humanitarian community, deepening divides between those "organizations working in the region and those lobbying for it from the outside" (Foley 2008, 11). Regarding the use of force, supporters were generally at odds over the proper response to the conflict. Aid providers rested on the possibility of a negotiated peace settlement, while more hawkish wings of the Save Darfur movement urged, from the outset, for an intervention of some sort—either by a multilateral, UN-sanctioned force, or even through unilateral action if necessary. "The tension between aid and advocacy is not unique to the Darfur conflict, though it is almost always papered over by the code of silence that governs relations among nonprofit groups" (Strom and Polgreen 2007). The public nature of this tussle is a testament to the high profile of the cause and of the actors.

Despite the hostility, however, "the relationship [was] also symbiotic" (Strom and Polgreen 2007). Aid groups benefit a great deal from the work of advocacy groups in making an issue out of what would otherwise be an overlooked crisis. Without the advertising and the celebrities, Darfur would be just another African disaster. However, between the GAO report, condemnation by the British advertising board, and deepening tensions among allies, stakeholders began to question whether this advertising campaign had served the interests of the organizations involved and the cause at the center of it all. David Rubenstein was forced to resign his post at the Save Darfur Coalition in June, replaced eventually by founding member Jerry Fowler (Strom and Polgreen 2007).

The surge of Save Darfur attracted both positive and negative attention, all as a product of the sheer volume of the Save Darfur brand. The Coalition's efforts lacked the quiet demeanor of humanitarianism; thus humanitarians felt as if their work was being compromised or threatened by this external actor. The Coalition's garish accusations of genocide provoked the furor of Sudan's sympathizers who stood up to push back on the verity of SDC's claims, with some success. Hulking into every room, Save Darfur's interests to present itself as the center of the movement were directly at odds with a savvier advocacy strategy that may have avoided these various pitfalls. I contend that the role played by the imperative to brand and market the cause was pursued at the expense of actual movement-building. The movement itself, as it was constituted by actual individual supporters, was mere window-dressing for an advertising campaign designed to suffice as political action. The branding of Save Darfur, stubbornly dependent on the bumper sticker conception of genocide, created a veneer to project an image of a mass movement. The appearance of support for genocide prevention through the Coalition's marketing was intended to give the impression to elite decision makers that there would be costs to inaction, just as the lessons from Rwanda were supposed to teach us. However, when the advertising efforts failed in this regard, there was no firm movement to follow-through on the claims of the organization. When pressuring politicians and financiers through marketing failed to stop violence in Darfur, the social movement shortcuts were laid bare and it became obvious that there would be no material consequences.

Save Darfur: The Brand

By 2007, pride in the brand was expressed in the letter soliciting for candidates to serve as the new executive director: "In three years, the name, 'Save Darfur,' has become the brand for the Darfur anti-genocide movement" (quoted in Mamdani 2009, 23). In creating the student organization, STAND "produced something of lasting value—a brand name" (Hamilton and Hazlett 2007, 3345). Throughout much of the literature and journalistic coverage of the movement, this kind of language is repeated as a strength for its capacity to breed familiarity and legitimacy. In the same way, consumers recognize cereal box cartoon characters, Save Darfur desired recognition as the preeminent and most trustworthy organization on atrocities prevention. Boiling down the crisis to fit onto a bumper sticker was a key tactic, a point articulated by David Rubenstein, founder of the Save Darfur Coalition: "...we realized that the closer we could get to a bumper sticker, the better we'd be as an organization" (Quoted in Hamilton and Hazlett 2007, 344). Nick Kristof, an early and prominent figure in the communication of the Darfur brand, complained that individuals were more likely to feel sympathy for "a suffering puppy with big eyes and floppy ears" than for human victims of violence (Kristof 2007). However, in certain terms, the label of genocide was the "Darfur puppy" (Crilly 2010, 167). It prefigured the way the audience would feel about the conflict and presumed a certain response. Genocide is unmatched in its reputation as the crime of all crimes and invoking that reputation was central to Save Darfur's branding strategy. Journalists, as powerful conjurers of public opinion, latched onto "genocide" for use as a headline. Broadcasters could repeat the label in a quick bite. "Stop Genocide" looks better on a t-shirt than "Stop this Confusing Conflict between Groups Whose Interests We Do Not Fully Understand, in which Thousands of People Are Dying of Diarrhea."

The chasm between the actual facts and the advertised facts is confounding and cannot reasonably be determined to have been simply a giant mistake. Branding the movement created a context in which numbers could be stretched, which also suggests that the actual facts were seen to be insufficient to motivate citizens to action. Deaths from diarrhea and malaria are not as sexy or glamorous as deaths from armed ethnic conflict. While 200,000 dead people by any means sound like a catastrophe, unrevised tallies of 400,000 remained on posters long after the numbers had been refuted. In these cynical times, when consumers have come to expect a certain level of duplicity from companies trying to sell products and increase market share, even the most jaded among us does not expect exaggeration on this scale from a high-profile human rights organization. We assume accuracy and credibility from those groups working to address moral causes, and we expect not to be taken advantage of by actors fighting the good fight.

Branded advertising emerges out of corporate competition as the outward expression of monopoly capitalism. To rise above the ebbs and flows of the market and situate themselves as indispensable ingredients to the postmodern lifestyle, commercial firms associate their products and services with persistent brand recognition. In an environment saturated with advertising, brand recognition provides certainty: "the brand becomes a symbol of confidence for the consumer, and a commitment to quality… [there is a] contractual dimension of the brand" (Chevalier and Mazzalovo 2004, 10). Branding insists on thorough, reliable uniformity, which in turn attracts and demands loyalty from the consumer base. Brand confidence is bred socially and culturally—by developing a reputation and an association tied to status. Louis Vuitton exudes luxury. Disney is fun and family oriented. Nike represents athletic prowess. Chanel embodies glamor and grace. However, lack of confidence is also bred culturally. From the Ford Pinto to the Exxon Valdez, negatively branded products and events are emblazoned with corporate names that remind consumers of harm to personal safety or ecological recklessness, for instance. When disparaging associations become attached to a brand, it is re-branded—re-cast as that which it wants to be, rather than that which it is or has been. Image and perception are the paramount goals of branding, not accuracy or faithfulness to reality.

The name, the logo, and the slogan are each essential components of contemporary brands. In the twenty-first century, brand names are short words with few syllables that place the corporation in the future, leaving behind its human, familial origins or merged and consolidated past. A logo is the graphic representation of the corporation designed to visually communicate meaning and transmit familiarity. With crisp contours and vivid color schemes, the logo is often more recognizable than the brand name, as it is plastered on sponsored items without the name present at all. For its prominence, the logo is "the heraldic shield of modern times," or the family crest of the firm (Chevalier and Mazzalovo 2004, 32). Finally, a slogan is the fullest articulation of the brand, synthesizing the message behind the name and logo. The projected identity is formalized with a mantra: "Just do it"; "The real thing"; "Think different"; "Reach out and touch someone"; "You've come a long way, baby!" Exemplifying assertiveness, authenticity, nonconformity, connectedness, and empowerment, each of these slogans are (ostensibly) attractive qualities that consumers desire to possess. The implication of corporate branding relies on the fastening of commodities to the euphoric experiences, sensations, and emotions portrayed in its advertising. Commodities become not what we own, but who we are. In place of ethics or values or other subcutaneous identity markers that constitute our selves, consumers are constituted by their purchases and possessions.

But, at the same time, this implication is neither directly stated nor actually intended. Even ad executives know that simple commodity items do not ensure happiness, high self-esteem, or emancipation; a broader, savvier agenda is at work. Possessions become key elements of a robust, actualized lifestyle. Consumer capitalism evolved to package its products as components of an ethereal commodity existence. "The old paradigm had it that all marketing was selling a product. In the new model… the selling of the brand acquired an extra component that can only be described as spiritual" (Klein 1999, 21). In order to sell a product as if it were a lifestyle or an experience, the branding must be robust. The interplay of the logo and slogan and the deployment of an advertising campaign are the tangible components to a fundamentally cultural appeal. As Starbucks founder Howard Schultz readily admits, "the real goal is 'to establish emotional ties'" (quoted in Barber 2007, 179). To forge connections between the psychological and the material is to craft an image of the product that rises above its instrumental value or even its status attribution; the goal being "to take these associations out of the representational realm and make them a lived reality" (Klein 1999, 29). After the product has been replaced by a projection of the branded lifestyle that the product brings into existence, the final sleight, then, is to have consumers transform into advertisements themselves. This is the force of branding: when this spectacular illusion has been created, the participants perpetuate its momentum by trafficking in the logos and slogans through the clothing they wear, the places they shop, the cars the drive, and the devices they use—living and breathing, walking and talking viral marketing.

The question remains, however, how this relates to human rights advocacy. If branding is an effective means of communication, then the tactic might carry over into other realms that have a need for the transmission of messages. One could reasonably anticipate the desire to embed meaning and identity within a political movement, so as to cultivate commitment and solidarity among its supporters. With this affiliation, a movement could assert itself and continue to broaden its constituency. However, there is a significant element of façade, of untruth, and of duplicity in advertising that might not be welcome or appropriate in a political movement's outreach campaign. Coke is not actually "the real thing" by any measure of reality; AT&T provides the ability to only figuratively "reach out and touch someone"; and by co-opting feminism, Virginia Slims is actually demonstrating how far women have *not* come, baby.

While a degree of tongue-and-cheek wordplay can be tolerated in the advertising world, this approach has a tenuous relationship to politics. Certainly, in election campaigns, candidates present themselves as that which they wish they were, or that as which they wish to be seen, branding themselves as a reformer, a maverick, or a stalwart defender of the past. Yet, in human rights campaigning, achieving legitimacy depends on the correlation between the messaging and the truth; they must be one and the same. When this imperative is sacrificed or lost unintentionally, the claim to moral authority vanishes and with it the power of human rights advocacy evaporates as well. Rather than relying on steadfast research, verified evidence, and first-hand testimony to carry their reputation, Save Darfur designed an image and crafted a brand to transcend traditional methodologies and anchor human rights advocacy in the hearts and minds of the masses.

Furthermore and finally, the false associations created through branding were those that carried Save Darfur from its infancy through its prime. The movement glimmered for a moment in 2004–2005 among high school students and churchgoers, but in the accelerated phase of 2006–2007, the movement was supplanted by a hologram of itself. Instead of solidarity with Sudanese civilians and direct action against the perpetrators, Save Darfur glistened as a bright, polished marketing scheme devoid of substance and increasingly divorced from facts. At this point, the branding was complete. Instead of building a permanent constituency for atrocities prevention, the SDC was removed from the shelf at the end of the aisle and gently moved into the discount bin, eclipsed by the next big product rollout.

Conclusion: Sharing Means Caring

Save Darfur's rise exemplifies a model for human rights advocacy adaptive to new technology and hyper-aware of the cultural context in which it operates. The move toward branding and cross-platform media presence recognizes how marketing is conducted in an age of corporate capitalism—deploying advertising devices for human rights ends. However problematic this transposition may be, the campaigns and their public profile elevated human rights further still. And as savvy as Save Darfur was in the areas of media and culture, the Coalition was just a few years ahead of its time. Assembling an email list of millions of subscribers and circulating online petitions stretched evolving technology as far as it could go but remained limited by the broadcast format of sending information in one direction to a receptive audience. A more profoundly realized version emerged in 2012 that capitalized on social media's network structure and culture of sharing: Invisible Children's campaign to make Joseph Kony famous.

With the past as prologue, the Kony 2012 campaign graced the covers of major magazines, the ledes of cable news shows, the wrists of high school students, and the lips of elected officials, all in the flash of a moment. Invisible Children (IC) provoked an outburst of public awareness of the crimes of the Lord's Resistance Army with the release of a thirty-minute YouTube video. The video was viewed 200,000 times by the end of official Los Angeles premiere and one million times within the first twenty-four hours. The force of the strategy that propelled Kony 2012 was its understanding and utilization of Web 2.0: digital social platforms provide the infrastructure for transmitting information at an exponential rate. By targeting "culture makers" and "policymakers," the organization was able to piggyback on the pre-existing fame of celebrities and other prominent figures. The name "Joseph Kony" spread with unprecedented contagion. Kony 2012 was the logical extension and perfect culmination of all that preceded it—entertainment, spectacle, and branding—and is also susceptible to all the same critiques.

The video opens with a wide aerial shot of the earth rotating as the first glimpse of the sun spills over the top of the horizon: "Humanity's greatest desire is to belong and to connect…We share what we love and it reminds us what we all have in common…and this connection is changing the way the world works." Oozing with cyber-utopian sentimentality, the voiceover expresses a central doctrine of the era of Twitter and Tumblr. Technological tools had finally caught up to a core human desire that can only now be fulfilled: seeing, sharing, connecting. The cosmopolitan aspirations of neoliberal globalization were realized; the moment of singularity in which the digital and the ethical become one. But, this is more than the lofty daydreaming of human rights defenders. This is also more than progressive pontification or wishful thinking. Rather, today's digital media luminaries speak exactly in these terms, not as an optimistic vision of tomorrow, but as a description of processes that are already within reach.

In his letter to shareholders and market observers ahead of Facebook's Initial Public Offering, CEO Mark Zuckerberg proclaimed his company's mission: "People sharing more…creates a more open culture and leads to a better understanding of the lives and perspectives of others. We believe that this creates a greater number of stronger relationships between people, and that it helps people get exposed to a greater number of diverse perspectives" (Ard 2012). The capacity to share information removes barriers to mutual understanding and is directly responsible for an awareness and appreciation of diversity. Zuckerberg continues with more overtly political language: "We believe building tools to help people share can bring a more honest and transparent dialogue around government that could lead to more direct empowerment of people, more accountability for officials and better solutions to some of the biggest problems of our time" (Ard 2012). This is a comment on the technological platform itself as a tool for people to apprehend their own democratic dreams, together.

The Kony 2012 video makes explicit reference to insurgent movements including Occupy Wall Street and the Arab Spring, images of Tahrir Square with men wrapped in keffiyeh scarves and handwritten cardboard banners, dodging tear gas canisters, as has become the familiar visual trope. The film then scrolls through news clips of stodgy old men nervously defending the status quo, fearing the coming anarchical collapse. Invisible Children see themselves in this light: as the stewards and torchbearers of a new disruptive global activism and a grassroots surge of youthful determination with the goal of upending elites. Yet, despite this self-image, Kony 2012 trades in the tired clichés that plague Western advocacy and further retrench power differentials: paternalism, racism, militarism, and a predictable obsession with themselves.

The film's stars are Invisible Children's co-founder and Chief Creative Officer Jason Russell, his son Gavin, and former LRA abductee and child soldier Jacob Acaye. The narrative revolves around Russell explaining to his son about IC's work through the impact that Kony has had on Jacob's life. Russell first encountered Jacob in his first trip to Uganda on a filmmaking expedition after college, the genesis of the organization and its mission. Jacob has since moved to the US and is a family friend of the Russells'. Gavin describes his dad's work: "you stop the bad guys from being mean," which is not wrong of course. The peculiarity of this storytelling device lies in the assumption that the conflict in central Africa can be adequately explained to a toddler—or that the human horror of the violence *should* be shared with a toddler. The interactions between Jason and Gavin are intended to communicate to the audience that the story really is this simple: even a toddler can understand what is at stake and why it is essential to be active in the fight for Kony's arrest and prosecution. As the film unfolds, the subject shifts from Gavin and Jacob to "you," the viewer, and the throngs of others you will join in protest once you make a commitment to this cause.

Yet, Jason Russell remains the deliberate focal point. His handsome features and compelling style draw us in as an audience. Brought up in the Christian theater company his parents started, Russell possesses an animated quality that suits him for the stage. Filmmaker and star, Russell operates behind and in front of the camera, the subject of his own opus. In important ways, this method of storytelling—in which the advocate takes center stage instead of victims/survivors or perpetrators—is an increasingly more present feature of the contemporary human rights landscape. The "humanitarian carnival" compels celebrities to become humanitarians *and* drives humanitarians to seek celebrity status (De Waal 2008). Charismatic leadership is one thing but fame/infamy is quite another.

Russell's is a cautionary tale in this regard. Ten days after Kony 2012 goes viral, Russell appears to succumb to the pressure brought on by the spotlight. TMZ.com, a celebrity website specializing in scandal, airs mobile phone footage of Russell, nude on a San Diego street corner and acting erratically, in the midst of a personal crisis brought on by the exhaustion and weight of the campaign. Russell was temporarily hospitalized to allow himself time to recover and returned to lead the organization (Perry 2012). His reemergence was facilitated in a manner that awkwardly mirrors a star's resurfacing following a stint in rehab: a *mea culpa* and public reckoning, with stops on the Today Show loveseat and Oprah's couch.

In the interview with Oprah, Jason Russell describes a "tsunami" of response to the video that demanded of him relentless cross-country travel to conduct seventeen interviews in 48 hours. Invisible Children was insufficiently staffed or otherwise prepared to handle the incessant media requests that accompanied the video's launch. In his capacity as spokesperson, Russell confronted not only the supportive reactions to the video, but the criticism as well, much of which, he felt, was directed at him personally. The positive and negative attention grew into an onslaught of stress and burden that boiled over into an unfortunately public breakdown. And, frankly, despite the sad impact of the video on Russell's mental health, it is difficult not to connect the meltdown to his and IC's strategic choices during the video production process. In the early 1990s, Human Rights Watch consciously avoided using spokespersons when it released reports, because the organization did not want the story to be about the messenger; the research would have to speak for itself if it was going to resonate. Twenty years later, tried and true advocacy strategies have been turned on their head.

The very notion that Kony's (or Russell's) fame would result in an arrest and prosecution by the International Criminal Court relies on a host of unusual assumptions that either ignores or actively challenges traditional approaches to human rights advocacy. Instead of relying on the fortitude on research and reporting, Invisible Children creates motivational films to drive fund-raising and mobilization. Kony 2012 was only one among dozens. Additionally, IC is active on the ground mostly in Uganda assisting local partners to track the movement of LRA personnel, encourage defection, and rehabilitate and reintegrate kidnapped children. They do not utilize naming and shaming strategies at all. They leverage public awareness in elite lobbying efforts that have won them small victories. Invisible Children throws dance parties and cultivates an active YouTube channel of new and emerging musicians. Equal parts marketing firm, social service, fraternity, and prayer circle. Its leaders are driven as if by calling to build a broad movement of young people attracted to the cause for its cultural prestige and projection of cool and fun. Invisible Children wants to be taken seriously not for its moral authority or for its ability to speak truth to power, but because it represents the will of lots and lots of people.

As the ideal manifestation of a mass appeal, Invisible Children's tactics amazingly and succinctly express many of the most prevalent objections to Western human rights. What Makau Mutua called the Savages–Victims–Saviors metaphor (2001), reacting to Kony 2012 Teju Cole calls the White-Savior-Industrial Complex (2012). Nearly synonymous, these tropes cast the white, Western human rights advocate as the crusader, which posits the other as the helpless and backward. Each "validates privilege" in Cole's words and reproduces pre-existing inequalities. African victims reprise their roles as colonial possessions to be improved, all of whom are treated like children whether or not they actually are children.

My sense is that Invisible Children is more an exception than a rule, for now. There are clear and problematic tendencies within many advocacy organizations to rely on American might, to desire military power, to proceed arrogantly, to pursue opportunistically, and to act without accountability for its interventions. But the influence of Kony 2012 on the human rights sector may compel fledgling NGOs seeking to break through to chase after a viral splash, rather than building their identities and their operations slowly and cautiously, in the mold of Amnesty International or Human Rights Watch. Kony 2012 preeminently privileges form over content. Invisible Children was constantly accused of trading in faulty facts and glossing over crucial evidence: Was Kony in Uganda? Was Kony even alive? Was LRA still active in kidnapping and child soldiering? Were there still children sleeping on the streets of Goma and North Kivu? It was more important that the priority of making Kony famous spoke for itself, evading these kinds of details. It would even be preferable for the audience not to ask questions at all, distracted by the MTV-style video editing and edgy dance music soundtrack. This strain of human rights advocacy cultivates uncritical engagement: followers prancing and twirling behind the pied piper, neatly in queue singing along, but never changing the tune or challenging the melody or improvizing new steps.

With posters, stickers, yard signs, fliers, and bracelets, all contained in an Action Kit available for purchase, Kony 2012 culminates on April 20, 2012 in an event entitled, "Cover the Night," in which supporters are tasked to "blanket every street in every city" with Joseph Kony's name and face. Rather than political action, we have yet another advertising campaign that relies on a magical trigger to set off a chain reaction of events to result in the arrest and extradition of a most notorious war criminal. The mechanism for IC is the same as it was for Darfur: masses stand in for an actualized movement and utilized to leverage face-to-face lobbying of elected officials. The appearance of a grassroots base is a low-cost, high-impact alternative to actually cultivating a grassroots base.

This instrumental approach to human rights advocacy operates comfortably within the social and technological confines of the early twenty-first century. The trends exhibited in Save Darfur continue and multiply in Kony 2012. Human rights is a lifestyle brand to flash around on t-shirts and bumper stickers, but now online networks constitute a heightened social environment in which to perform support for causes and issues. Rather than relying on advertising in public spaces like billboards and train stations, through digital social networks, marketers package their content for maximum virality, send it out, and wait for end users to do the work for them. Therefore, when a brand diffuses rapidly over a short period of time, it appears as though the spread is natural and organic when in fact it is all the product of an elaborate public relations trick. Kony 2012 is merely another product in this likeness. Kony 2012 is an adaptation, not a transformation. Corporate culture with new digital toys elevated the possibility while constraining the potential. Twenty-first-century mass appeals are little more than a rebranding: new look, same old product.

Notes

1. Interview, November 4, 2014.
2. Interview, November 4, 2014.
3. Interview, November 4, 2014.
4. The analysis of the financial standing and expenses of the SDC in this section is based on calculations by the author of the publically available Forms 990 submitted to the US Internal Revenue Service, 2004–2009.
5. Interview, November 4, 2014.
6. Titles include *The Media and Darfur: Sensationalism and Irresponsibility*; *The Extremist Roots of the Darfur Rebellion*; and *Darfur, Human Rights and Hypocrisy* and all are available free of charge via download from ESPAC's Web site. Hoile is a notorious figure in British conservative politics with a history of support for authoritarian cold war regimes in Angola, Mozambique, and Nicaragua (Rose 1986). As a leader of the Federation of Conservative Students in the mid-1980s, Hoile was condemned by members of the Tory party for his extremism and infamously wore a "Hang Mandela" sticker, while Mandela was imprisoned on Robben Island (Borger 2007).

References

Amnesty International. 2003a. "Sudan: Urgent Call for Commission of Inquiry in Darfur as Situation Deteriorates." AFR 54/004/2003. London.

———. 2003b. "Sudan: Crisis in Darfur—Urgent Need for International Commission of Inquiry and Monitoring." AFR 54/026/200. London.

Ard, Scott. 2012. "Mark Zuckerberg's IPO Letter: Why Facebook Exists." *Yahoo! Finance*, February 1. http://finance.yahoo.com/news/mark-zuckerberg-ipo-letter–why-facebook-exists.html.

Barber, Benjamin R. 2007. *Consumed: How Markets Corrupt Children, Infantilize Adults, and Swallow Citizens Whole*. New York: W. W. Norton.

BBC. 2007. "World Rallies for Darfur Action." *BBC*, April 29. http://news.bbc.co.uk/2/hi/6604555.stm.

Borger, Julian. 2007. "Darfur by Numbers." *The Guardian*, September 4.

Bush, Michael. 2010. "Weber Shandwick Is No. 9 on Ad Age's Agency A-List." *Advertising Age*, January 25. http://adage.com/agencya-list09/article?article_id=141694.

Cheadle, Don, and John Prendergast. 2007. *Not on Our Watch: The Mission to End Genocide in Darfur and Beyond*. New York: Hyperion.

Chevalier, Michel, and Gerald Mazzalovo. 2004. *Pro Logo: Brands as a Factor of Progress*. Houndmills, UK: Palgrave Macmillan.

Christian Solidarity International. 2017. "About Us." https://csi-usa.org/about-us/.

Cole, Teju. 2012. "The White-Savior Industrial Complex." *The Atlantic*, March 21. http://www.theatlantic.com/international/archive/2012/03/the-white-savior-industrial-complex/254843.

Committee of Conscience. 2000. "United States Holocaust Memorial Museum's Committee on Conscience Takes Action to Raise Public Awareness of Sudan Genocide Threat." Washington, DC: United States Holocaust Memorial Museum.

———. 2004. "United States Holocaust Memorial Museum Emphasizes Threat of Genocide in Sudan." Washington, DC: United States Holocaust Memorial Museum.

Corey, Charles W. 2004. "US Congress Terms Situation in Darfur 'Genocide'." US State Department press release, July 23.

Crilly, Rob. 2010. *Saving Darfur: Everyone's Favorite African War*. London: Reportage.

Dallaire, Roméo. 2004. *Shake Hands with the Devil: The Failure of Humanity in Rwanda*. New York: Da Capo Press.

De Waal, Alex. 2008. "The Humanitarian Carnival: A Celebrity Vogue." *World Affairs* 171 (2): 43–56.

Eichler-Levine, Jodi, and Rosemary Hicks. 2007. "'As Americans' Against 'Genocide': The Crisis in Darfur and Interreligious Political Activism." *American Quarterly* 59 (3): 711–35.

Fake, Steven, and Kevin Funk. 2009. *Scramble for Africa: Darfur-Intervention and the USA*. Montreal: Black Rose Books.

Flint, Julie, and Alex De Waal. 2008. *Darfur: A New History of a Long War*. Revised and Updated edition. African Arguments. London: Zed Books.

Foley, Conor. 2008. *The Thin Blue Line: How Humanitarianism Went to War*. London: Verso.

Guha-Sapir, Debarati, and Olivier Degomme. 2005. "Darfur: Counting the Deaths." Brussels: Centre for Research on the Epidemiology of Disaster. http://www.cred.be/sites/default/files/DarfurCountingtheDeaths.pdf.

Hamilton, Rebecca. 2011. *Fighting for Darfur: Public Action and the Struggle to Stop Genocide*. Palgrave Macmillan.
Hamilton, Rebecca, and Chad Hazlett. 2007. "'Not On Our Watch': The Emergence of the American Movement for Darfur." In *War in Darfur and the Search for Peace*, edited by Alex De Waal, 337–66. Cambridge, MA: Harvard University Press.
Human Rights Watch. 2010. "Sudan: ICC Warrant for Al-Bashir on Genocide." Human Rights Watch, July 13. https://www.hrw.org/news/2010/07/13/sudan-icc-warrant-al-bashir-genocide.
International Crisis Group. 2003. "Sudan's Other Wars." Africa Briefing No. 14. Khartoum and Brussels.
Klein, Naomi. 1999. *No Space, No Choice, No Jobs, No Logo: Taking Aim at the Brand Bullies*. New York: Picador.
Kristof, Nicholas D. 2004. "Ethnic Cleansing, Again." *New York Times*, March 24. http://www.nytimes.com/2004/03/24/opinion/ethnic-cleansing-again.html.
———. 2007. "Save the Darfur Puppy." *The New York Times*, May 10. http://select.nytimes.com/2007/05/10/opinion/10kristof.html.
Lanz, David. 2009. "Save Darfur: A Movement and Its Discontents." *African Affairs* 108 (433): 669–677.
M+R Strategic Services. 2011. "Save Darfur Coalition." http://www.mrss.com/strategic-communications/case-studies/save-darfur-coalition.
Mamdani, Mahmood. 2007. "The Politics of Naming: Genocide, Civil War, Insurgency." *London Review of Books* 29 (5): 8.
———. 2009. *Saviors and Survivors: Darfur, Politics, and the War on Terror*. New York: Pantheon Books.
Mutua, Makau. 2001. "Savages, Victims, and Saviors: The Metaphor of Human Rights." *Harvard International Law Journal* 42 (1): 201–45.
Perry, Tony. 2012. "Jason Russell: Neighbors Tried to Calm Him As He Acted 'Bizarre.'" *LA Times Blogs—L.A. NOW* (blog), March 16. http://latimesblogs.latimes.com/lanow/2012/03/jason-russell-kony-2012-invisible-children.html.
Power, Samantha. 2007. *"A Problem from Hell": America and the Age of Genocide*. New York: Harper Perennial.
Preston, Caroline. 2006. "Grandson of Holocaust Survivors Rallies Support for Darfur." *Chronicle of Philanthropy*, June 29.
Prunier, Gérard. 2007. *Darfur: The Ambiguous Genocide*. Revised and Updated edition. Ithaca, NY: Cornell University Press.
Reeves, Eric. 2003. "The Face of War in Darfur (Sudan): Many Tens of Thousands Flee Khartoum's Campaign of Aerial Bombardment, Militia Attacks." October 8. http://www.sudanreeves.org/Sections-article285-p1.html.

Rose, David. 1986. "Right Wing Tightens Group on Students and Scorns Inquiry." *The Guardian*, April 3.

Save Darfur Coalition. 2004. "Unity Statement." July 14. http://savedarfur.org/pages/unity_statement.

———. 2006. "Musical Groups Big & Rich and O.A.R. to Appear at 'Save Darfur Now: Voices to End Genocide' Rally in New York City's Central Park on September 17." Save Darfur. http://savedarfur.org/musical-groups-big-rich-o-r-appear-save-darfur-now-voices-end-genocide-rally-new-york-citys-central-park-september-17.

———. 2011. "Global Campaigns." http://savedarfur.org/pages/global_campaigns.

Straus, Scott. 2005. "Darfur and the Genocide Debate." *Foreign Affairs*, February.

Strom, Stephanie, and Lydia Polgreen. 2007. "Advocacy Group's Publicity Campaign on Darfur Angers Relief Organizations." *The New York Times*, June 2.

Sudhaman, Arun. 2014. "Edelman, Weber Shandwick, Then Daylight." *Holmes Report* (blog), July 7. http://worldreport.holmesreport.com/top-10.

Thomas-Jensen, Colin, and Julia Spiegel. 2008. "Activism and Darfur: Slowly Driving Policy Change." *Fordham International Law Journal* 31 (4): 843.

United States Government Accountability Office. 2006. "Darfur Crisis: Death Estimates Demonstrate Severity of Crisis, But Their Accuracy and Credibility Could Be Enhanced." GAO-07-24.

Vargas, Jose Antonio. 2006. "In 'Darfur Is Dying,' The Game That's Anything But." *Washington Post*, May 1, sec. C.

Vennochi, Joan. 2007. "Divestment Dilemma." *Boston.Com*, May 10. http://www.boston.com/news/globe/editorial_opinion/oped/articles/2007/05/10/divestment_dilemma/.

Zengerle, Jason. 2006. "Student Aid." *The New Republic*, March 27. http://www.tnr.com/article/politics/student-aid.

CHAPTER 6

Reclaiming Human Rights as a Politics of Resistance

On February 5, 2014, Amnesty International USA, held yet another massive benefit concert, this time at the Barclays Center in Brooklyn. Equal parts 1980s nostalgia and twenty-first-century flare, Bringing Human Rights Home was an attempt at a reboot in an era of stagnation. Performers that evening consisted of an odd mix of flash-in-the-pan pop artists and cult favorites, flanked by a handful of humanitarian mainstays. Appearances by Yoko Ono, Peter Gabriel, and Sting elicited familiarity and contextualized the event for older audiences. And no spectacle of this magnitude would be complete without the crown prince himself, Bob Geldof, whose head of white feathery hair glowed under the arena lights. Geldof performed his thirty-year-old one-hit wonder, "I Don't Like Mondays," a song with little resonance for the youthful crowd, but provided historical gravitas to the occasion. More hotly anticipated than "I Don't Like Mondays" were two special guests making their American debut, recently released from a Russian prison camp: Nadezhda "Nadya" Tolokonnikova and Maria "Masha" Alekhina.

Nadya and Masha were two of the three members of the feminist art collective known as Pussy Riot who served an extended sentence after being convicted of hooliganism and public disruption by courts acting at the behest of Vladimir Putin. The women attracted global attention and their incarceration prompted the designation of Prisoner of Conscience from Amnesty, a *nom de guerre* assigned to cases adopted by the NGO

J. R. Pruce, *The Mass Appeal of Human Rights*, Human Rights Interventions, https://doi.org/10.1007/978-3-319-92075-7_6

signifying violations of freedom of expression. Pussy Riot represented the resistance against Putin's belligerent policies, domestic, regional, and international. Outsiders opportunistically seized on the issue, leveraging the publicity to score geopolitical points and advance their own agendas; Amnesty International can be counted among them.

The transformation and appropriation of Pussy Riot into global human rights icons took many forms. Pussy Riot's unmistakably vivid, polychromatic balaclavas were plastered across Web sites and campaign posters. Nadya was photographed on her way into a court hearing early on in this episode wearing a blue t-shirt with yellow lettering that read "no pasaràn" joined by the stenciled graphic of a raised closed fist.[1] Amnesty also produced "Free Pussy Riot" merchandise that utilized a recognizable font made famous by CBGBs, the legendary punk rock venue in downtown Manhattan on Bowery Street that birthed, among others, The Ramones and Blondie. Pussy Riot emerges from punk and riot grrrl counter-cultures and self-identifies with this legacy. Yet, the subversive elements of Pussy Riot's politics and aesthetics become dislocated as they are translated, filtered, and packaged for mass appeal.

Madonna introduces the anarchists-turned superstars: "I am honored to introduce my fellow freedom fighters Masha and Nadya from Pussy Riot. I have admired their courage and have long supported their commitment and the sacrifices they have made in the name of freedom of expression and human rights" (Amnesty International USA 2014). As the "Material Girl" speaks, rather than coalesce and converge, universes collide: human rights advocacy and social protest, pop culture and punk rock, celebrities and provocateurs, spectacle and substance, branding and art, consumerism and anti-capitalism. The hegemony of human rights clings to the edginess of what Pussy Riot stands for and seeks to co-opt the group's radical currency. As a mainstream and orderly vision of global engagement, transnational human rights prefers to inhabit multiple spaces without prompting conflict or expressing contradiction. Human rights NGOs want to be palatable in order to attract the broadest demographic, while also posing challenges that threaten status quo ideologies about state power and economic distribution. Human rights actors want to have it both ways: to seem approachable as well as confrontational. Masha's and Nadya's inclusion as Amnesty spokespersons is only the most recent manifestation of this tension, but the various reactions to the concert question whether this balance is sustainable. The edifice of the human rights movement cracks and crumbles as its internal ironies materialize as political dilemmas.

The Pussy Riot affair produces strong new evidence that the tactics and strategies of the human rights community have run their course.

They are no longer attractive to the audience and demand rethinking, if the human rights idea is to persist in this mode. Critics in attendance at Bringing Human Rights Home recount a palpable sense of deflation and disappointment—"the night felt unpleasantly self-congratulatory"—that Amnesty was simply going through the motions, uninspired, desperately striving to reinvigorate its base, project cultural relevance, and validate its own reason for being, but falling flat (Frere-Jones 2014). Contemporaneous with their appearance at the Barclays Center, the other anonymous members of Pussy Riot disown Masha and Nadya, rejecting their role "as institutionalized advocates" remarking that "such advocacy is hardly compatible with radical political statements and provocative works of art" (Garadja et al. 2014). If this model of human rights advocacy fails to appeal to the audience, and as well does not offer any utility to the activists, then whose interests or purposes does it serve?

But even more that disapproval, Pussy Riot articulates a fundamental divide between the incendiary nature of social protest and the muted articulation of professional advocacy. This suggests that instead of serving as gatekeeper, benefactor, or force multiplier, major human rights NGOs may often act as a vacuum, sucking out the force and momentum from vibrant movements. The consequences of this determination would be significant and may possess the potential to prompt a process of soul-searching and critical self-reflection by the human rights community. Rather than considering how Masha and Nadya can be instrumental for Amnesty International's fund-raising prowess and public prestige, Amnesty International should explore the opportunity to learn from them and be shaped from below.

If human rights is a secular religion with faithful adherents devoted to the gospel (Hopgood 2006), then what the transnational human rights movement needs is a spiritual revival. Prophets, mystics, and muses are all around us, but they do not occupy offices in the Empire State Building in New York or on K Street in Washington, nor can they be found on Hollywood billboards or the weekly Top 40 pop charts. Human rights ideas are born of struggle, and in order to breathe new air into the lungs of a faltering movement, it becomes essential to reconnect practice to principle. This book attempts to capture how human rights ideas are regularly mediated by cultural and commercial filters and fundamentally altered as they are translated for mass consumption. In this final chapter, I propose a way forward to transcend the inherent tensions of mass appeals and reclaim human rights as a politics of resistance.

The Aura of Human Rights

To Walter Benjamin, "aura" signifies the essence of the thing. A spectator experiences aura when in the immediate, unmediated presence of art or nature. Recall a moment when you entered a room in a museum: cavernous vaulted ceilings, meticulous crown molding on the doorways and floorboards, parquet wood tiles. You turn a corner to be confronted by a piece hanging on the wall in front of you. You are at first struck by its size perhaps, then by the sheer force of its beauty, the colors, the textures, the composition, the figures. You stare at it as its aura washes over you. You get lost in its details and permit your imagination to wander through it. This is a visceral, nearly physical, experience witnesses share with inanimate objects, yet objects whose aesthetics bear meaning and carry significance. Similarly with natural beauty. Consider the momentary paralysis we feel when captivated by a bright pink sunset, the vast ocean, or awe-inspiring mountain scape. Aura connects the individual to the thing in a direct manner, opening pathways for sensation, interpretation, and engagement. Aura is pure and authentic. Aura expresses the "uniqueness of every reality" (Benjamin 1968, 223). For this reason, as images are reproduced with the use of new technologies and tools, their aura decays and fades, leaving only a residue and a faint afterglow of their true essence.

Pussy Riot represents the aura of human rights, a spirit that embraces deviance and celebrates originality. Pussy Riot embraces ingenuity and rejects predictability. Their public performances were rebellious flash mobs that by their nature challenge prevailing ideologies about decency, civility, and conformity. In a revealing and at times bizarre series of exchanges with cultural theorist Slavoj Žižek, from prison Nadya remarks on Pussy Riot's association with world-historical revolutionary forces whose purposes identified with "criticism, creativity and co-creation, experimentation and constantly provocative events" (Žižek and Tolokonnikova 2013). This perspective is at odds with mainstream human rights advocacy that has relied upon routinized strategies in the pursuit of recruitment and fund-raising. Benefit concerts and celebrities are central to this model. Juxtaposed against the outrageous musical displays of Pussy Riot in Russia, these mass events are antithetical to a radical aura. They are pre-programmed and highly centralized. The audience's reactions are anticipated and choreographed with carefully planned punch lines and tear-jerking moments. Fundamentally, mass events lack and even resist spontaneity. When Masha and Nadya appear on stage with Madonna in Brooklyn, they do so as mechanical reproductions of their former selves. They are packaged for the mass audience to symbolize the aura of human rights, yet all we are left with is a rotting appropriation of the radical.

The other members of Pussy Riot, still anonymous and still underground, were highly sensitive to this and made as much clear in their letter disowning Nadya and Masha:

> Institutionalised advocacy can hardly afford a critique of fundamental norms and rules that underlie modern patriarchal society. Being an institutional part of society, such advocacy cannot go beyond the rules set forth by this society... The mixing of the rebel feminist punk image with the image of institutionalised defenders of prisoners' rights is harmful to us as a collective, and harmful to the new role that Nadya and Masha have taken on. (Garadja et al. 2014)

The need to distance their cause and their identities from that of their former members and from Amnesty International signals a crucial separation between transnational human rights and sites of struggle. This sentiment describes an antagonism that many social movements and grassroots activists share with respect to major NGOs. Particularly among movements in the Global South, concern exists that Northern organizations do not reflect their values or, worse, possess agendas that may conflict with or trump their own.

Pussy Riot continues. "We, as an art collective, have an ethical right to preserve our art practice, our name and our visual identity, distinct from other organisations" (Garadja et al. 2014). Crucially, the members see their identity corrupted as advocacy groups co-opt their likenesses and their symbols. Pussy Riot seeks to recapture propriety over their identities, which have been seized by powerful actors without the full consent of the collective. Pussy Riot teaches us that there is an ethical imperative for identity, practice, and politics to be in agreement (the visual realm provides one context for this). Mass media and popular culture impact this intersection by tearing it apart. The aura or essence of Pussy Riot was compromised by the way in which it was trafficked and reproduced by actors outside the group.

Yet, Benjamin also believed contra, his Frankfurt School brethren that mass culture possessed a revolutionary potential, albeit often unrealized. Pussy Riot are not luddites. They are twenty-first-century political operatives, meaning they take advantage of modern technology for political purposes. Their performances were spontaneous to the live audience, but were also devised and staged so as to have maximum impact. Performances were as crafted for the live demonstration as they were for their lives in perpetuity, online. Their events were videotaped, edited, and then released on the Web for a global audience. It is certainly true that the videos are mechanical reproductions of the live performance, but are not merely vacuous duplications; they contained critical messaging that becomes amplified the more the videos circulate. Even from a prison camp, Pussy Riot's activism spread virally as millions and millions of people viewed their videos. Footage from the church on the fateful day of their arrest was rebroadcast in news productions, each time chipping away at the veneer of Putin's total control. Their videos persist with aura deeply embedded.

Media production cannot be simply relegated to the category of decay because it employs technology. This misses Benjamin's point. There is a strong threat, given the capitalist structures within which mass media is produced, that hegemonic ideologies will drown out objectionable voices. Furthermore, the reproduction of images by mechanical means has a conditioning effect on the viewer. Rather than invite the spectator to engage with the image, reproductions assume and cultivate specific, passive responses. Yet, Pussy Riot teaches us that even in the age of mass spectacle, counterspectacles that possess the aura of human rights—a radical essence that insists on dignity and empowerment—remain a viable political option. Technology provides the tools for activists and advocates to produce and share media that provide alternative narratives and challenge status quo assumptions. "Benjamin's heirs have suggested how messages of dissent can emanate from the heart of the culture industry, particularly in giving voice to oppressed or marginalized groups" (Ross 2014). Rejecting popular forms of expression in favor of modes that cut against the grain is not a natural disposition for a mainstream human rights organization, but this new direction serves the future sustainability of a movement that too often falls into the same cultural traps.

Détournement and Disruption

Guy Debord and his band of merry Situationists conceptualize *détournement* as "the reuse of preexisting artistic elements in a new ensemble" and a general effort to check the encroachment of reactionary ideologies on cultural and social life (Knabb 2006, 67). "*Détournement* (literally 'diversion,' as in 'diverting the path of a stream') consisted of appropriating the products of popular and mass culture and, through physically altering them, turning their ideological subtext back upon themselves, and revealing their manipulative effects upon consciousness" (Erickson 1992, 46). This approach to politics understands that power is exercised and contested in the discursive terrain and sees art as a mode of resistance. But even art, in its performance, production, and presentation, bears the imprint of late-industrial capitalism and the hegemonic forces it engenders. Therefore, artists must conduct themselves defensively and offensively, protecting free expression and pushing the boundaries of public sensibility. Toward this end, *détournement* demands making audiences willingly and unwillingly uncomfortable. In its simplest form, *détournement* recycles objects and meanings in new contexts so as to give the viewer pause and prompt reflection.[2] As a disruptive artistic practice, *détournement* violates familiarity, invites disorder, and cultivates critique.

Pussy Riot is the second manifestation of the Russian art collective previously known as *Voina*, translated as "war." Voina consisted of university students who gathered together in 2009 as a response to the return of Vladimir Putin to the Prime Minister's office and what they saw as the continuing creep of oligarchy. This period witnesses significant public protest on a mass scale against Putin's vision for Russia, seen to be catering to elite interests at the expense of overlooked, suffering middle classes. These students took their own tact, embodying the Situationist ethic of *détournement*.

> Voina married politics and art—they threw live cats around a McDonald's to protest for workers' rights; staged an orgy in front of a bear at Moscow's natural history museum to protest the election of Dmitry Medvedev, whose last name derives from the Russian word for "bear"; and, in later years, drew a massive phallus on a drawbridge across from the security services' headquarters in St. Petersburg. (Elder 2014)

These sorts of pranks are not intended to have direct political impact, but rather to contest power in and through cultural and social spaces—to shake loose the public audience from their own complacency and signal to authorities that unrest is bubbling right beneath the surface.

Stunts and actions such as these are met with fierce violence and harsh judicial sentences. Police regularly stormed the homes that Voina and Pussy Riot occupied (at times squatting, unlawfully). "The cops laid Oleg and Lenya face down, tied their hands behind their backs and put plastic bags on their heads" (Ash 2011). In one incident, Voina produced a video in which a toddler kicks a soccer ball under a police car. A small group of activists run out and overturn the car, so as to return the ball to the child (Galperina 2010). Following their arrests, two Voina members were held for three months in facilities rampant with bed bugs and disease; their lawyer would subsequently file a claim with the European Court of Human Rights. World famous street artist Banksy posted bail for these activists, but their troubles did not end upon their release. After a press conference and on their way home, plain-clothes officials (or their proxies) followed the group in the street, awaiting provocation and responded with beatings. The child of a Voina member was injured after his head was smashed into a wall during the melee. The child's mother, Natalia Sokol, was dragged by her hair through the streets, tearing out braided locks. The state did not see these students as *merely* a disruption. Voina's strategy of "full frontal confrontation" rattled national and local authorities and bore significant personal risks to the activists' security and safety (Ash 2011).

Pussy Riot departs from Voina to constitute an all-female, feminist collective, while retaining the spirit and method of *détournement*. As a punk rock band, their actions revolved around playing music. The women rush into a space, carrying equipment, and immediately set up and start playing. Guerrilla style, Pussy Riot staged performances in specific venues to mock and chide elite culture: department stores, luxury car dealerships, and couture fashion shows. Themselves clad in colorful dresses, bright tights, and neon balaclavas that preserve their anonymity while expressing their feminism and femininity. Their songs carry political and social commentary, but more important than the content is the form.

The punk, oi!, and riot grrrl styles that inspire Pussy Riot are inherently abrasive. Songs are not melodic. Lyrics are not sung, but yelled and shouted. The women march around, moshing, kicking, and punching the air, in a somewhat coordinated fashion, but hardly rhythmic. Video renditions produced for the Web are over-dubbed with full song versions and edited for impact. Public actions give the appearance of spontaneity because the audience has not been made aware of what is about to happen, but in fact the performances are highly coordinated for immediate effect and for their online global audience.

Cultural expressions are not simply instrumental and communicative; in and of themselves, cultural products contest power in discursive space. This is why form matters. This is a crucial tenet that transnational human rights actors can learn from Pussy Riot: Art and aesthetics provide platforms for disrupting political privilege. However, art and aesthetics may also reinforce hierarchy and inequality to the extent they "ape the methods of the ruling classes," to employ Gramsci's penetrating language (Gramsci 1971, 232). By creating their own media and pushing it out across multiple spaces—terrestrial and digital, for instance—Pussy Riot teaches us that disruptive cultural practices have both inherent and pragmatic value for human rights struggle. For this reason, the collective took offense to the notion that Nadya and Masha would appear at Barclays Center, at a concert with very expensive tickets, flanked by wealthy pop stars, made possible by corporate media conglomerates, and sanctioned by the blessing of the state. "Our performances are always illegal, staged only in unpredictable locations and public places not designed for traditional entertainment. The distribution of our clips is always through free and unrestricted media channels" (Garadja et al. 2014). It is antithetical for Pussy Riot that a movement for human emancipation and dignity should cuddle so closely with structural forces determined to protect private interests and restrict individual freedom.

This is the core tension of the mass appeal: They justify their existence by arguing for their necessity. In order for shaming strategies and fund-raising drives to be effective, for example, human rights organizations must appeal to the broadest, basest constituency imaginable. In the process, mass media and popular culture become "indispensable" tools for outreach, recruitment, and general communication efforts. It is what the public knows and is familiar with. It is what we are used to seeing and hearing. The mass appeal is fashioned after commercials and marketing pitches, rather than as calls to action against injustice and abuse. Mass appeals "ape the methods" of consumer capitalism, undercutting the unrealized potential of the global human rights movement. Defeatists and conformists too frequently suggest that this is a game that must be played that there are no alternatives. But there *are* other options available to us that draw on principled stances rather than transactional decisions, if only we free ourselves from the constraints of habit and routine. Recapturing the radical aura of human rights through social practices that confront dominant culture and challenge status quo politics demands a new approach to transnational advocacy.

Refusing Instrumentality, Negating Opportunism

For Herbert Marcuse, "the Great Refusal" is the only way to resist the totally administered society (1964, 257). Hegemonic ideologies ingest alternative perspectives and regurgitate them as their own, as pacified, sanitized modes of politics. And as we engage in political contestation with pre-packaged methods, we deepen our alienation from ourselves, constrain the potential for solidarity with others, and strengthen structures of entrenched power. Individuals and groups that desire an alternative—an evolution of respect for dignity, democracy, and distribution—must recognize their roles in consolidating the very forces they oppose. Negative dialectical thinking and action are the only appropriate responses to a mass culture that has co-opted all available avenues for protest. Following Marcuse's praxis, the initial step is to negate the whole and develop indigenous methods and approaches to political struggle. "The fact that they start refusing to play the game may be the fact which marks the beginning of the end" (Marcuse 1964, 257).

From the perspective of a human rights advocacy organization, "playing the game" means survival in a deeply competitive environment of media, popularity, funding, and causes. After all, an assumption behind the whole premise of this book permits that NGOs and movements pursue mass appeal for the various benefits it provides. Splashy events, celebrity endorsements, mainstream news coverage, and branded advertising offer competitive advantages not only relative to other NGOs, but also in relation to everything else going on in the world that individuals are asked to care about. Cutting through the saturated environment is a key challenge facing even the largest and most recognizable NGOs, let alone start-ups or organizations based outside of the Western metropolis. Being successful in this world requires, in the current model, a significant amount of money and prestige and mass appeals have been a central strategic component of the human rights community throughout its history.

Precisely, this interaction propels the critical arguments throughout the book: Human rights as a moral approach to global politics is inherently situated in a material world of resource scarcity, cost–benefit analysis, and self-interest. Ideology confronts instrumentality. Opportunism tempts deontology. Principles clash with pragmatics. Advocacy organizations embody this paradoxical space, but they also succumb to it too often. Compromising the aura of human rights for the sake of operational demands may produce short-term gains, but risks long-term viability. The soul and foundation of a global human rights movement must be constituted by something more profound than insipid relationships forged through patterns of consumerism. Rejecting conventional wisdom about the necessity for mass appeals as a prerequisite for meaningful human rights advocacy first requires exploring its contradictions.

The night after the Amnesty International concert in Brooklyn, a fund-raising cocktail party was held at the Spotted Pig, an acclaimed Greenwich Village gastropub frequented by the city's elite (and the site of rampant sexual harassment and abuse against employees by management and patrons). Proceeds from the evening benefited the party's host, the VOICE Project, an American NGO focused on the rights of artists and activists to free expression. The VOICE Project was initially launched to support peace in central Africa by using art and music as communicative platforms. The organization was founded by Anna Gabriel, the daughter of Peter Gabriel, an alumnus of the 1980s Amnesty International benefit concerts (Flanary 2013). VOICE's first campaign sought to amplify the songs of mothers whose children were abducted by Joseph Kony's Lord's Resistance Army; for this program, VOICE partnered with Invisible Children (VOICE Project, n.d.). But on this February evening in 2014, VOICE celebrated its role in supporting the release of Masha and Nadya from a Russian prison camp. The VOICE Project commanded the international donor response to the trial of Pussy Riot. The organization raised $121,376.55 to cover a range of expenses related to the women's incarceration. Over $90,000 was devoted to "childcare, prisoner safety monitoring by local attorneys, family travel costs, ground support team expenses, food, clothes, supplies, and communication" (VOICE Project 2014). Additionally, over $15,000 went to the rest of the Pussy Riot collective. Significant amounts of money were spent on significant matters in the lives of human rights activists.

In attendance at the event were luminaries from the worlds of art, music, and film, including Kim Gordon of Sonic Youth, Questlove of the Roots, James Murphy of LCD Sound system, actor siblings Jake and Maggie Gyllenhaal, and performance artist Marina Abramovic (Shepherd 2014). The guest list as well as the guests of honor exuded a thick sense of hip. They had come to support the cause as well as to be photographed with or next to Masha and Nadya, who, for the moment, were fixed in the center of New York City's bright spotlight. But for artist and writer Molly Crabapple, an anxiety whispered through the dining rooms of the Spotted Pig; uneasiness at the absurdity of mass appeals:

> It's so easy to skewer these parties, though the cash they raise underpins life-and-death activism. Without rich people benefits, groups like Amnesty International would never be able to save real human beings from jail... But they have none of the feral beauty of Pussy Riot...There is nothing [sic] transcendent here. There is nothing untamed. The celebrities and celebrity-worship, the objectification and mass-media-simplification—they may be necessary, but they had little to do with the brave, brilliant women who stood squinting in the camera flash. (2014)

Masha and Nadya made brief remarks and attempted, as they regularly did on their American tour, to turn the media's attention to their new crusade for prison reform. However, nobody seemed at all concerned about mass incarceration, access to medical care, or overcrowding.

Pussy Riot was the main attraction as well as a sideshow. Thrust before a universe foreign to them, the two women were shuffled about all evening, ogled by onlookers, and posing for photographs with adoring fans. "Nadya and Masha were in this world but not of it" (Crabapple 2014). American publics consumed Pussy Riot, while applauding itself for their freedom. NGOs like VOICE and Amnesty earned street cred through their support of and affiliation with *real* activists. That week Masha and Nadya conducted interviews with everyone from Buzzfeed to Stephen Colbert, and participated in a closed-door meeting with US Ambassador to the UN, Samantha Power (Elder 2014). Whether or not they liked it, Pussy Riot had arrived.

And that was excellent news to the advocacy community even as it alienated the collective. Pussy Riot's release and appearance in the US splashed human rights headlines nationwide, elevating Amnesty's name once again. As well, Amnesty in particular triumphantly celebrated their work for Masha and Nadya, positing themselves as the indispensable center of the human rights universe—despite claims that Putin freed Pussy Riot as a political ploy ahead of the Sochi Olympics. But that didn't matter because in a competitive environment every win, every mention, and every check counts. The evening at the Spotted Pig, with flashbulbs crackling and champagne flutes clinking, the human rights movement took another step away from its principles and towards the abyss. "It was that whole siphon-money-out-of-rich-people dance that all effective activist organizations do, but not very punk rock" (Crabapple 2014).

Conclusion

At precisely this moment, in an age of consumerism, global human rights needs a strong dose of punk rock: resistant, resilient, radical. Amnesty International and other major transnational NGOs that rely on grassroots support must learn from activists like Pussy Riot and avoid the temptation to stand over, exploit, and co-opt. Refusing the transactional benefits of mass appeal demands finding alternate avenues for advocacy. Negating the elite world of celebrity and philanthropy requires reimagining the global human rights movement. Put simply, without a new vision for the future, human rights advocacy condemns itself to the certain legacy as a passing fad—a briefly fashionable expression of postmodern global identity, popular among college students and baby boomers.

Pussy Riot's actionism was never about any particular objective or campaign or culminating event, but about persistent struggle as a disruptive social force. "We are the rebels asking for the storm, and believing that truth is only to be found in an endless search" (Žižek and Tolokonnikova 2013). Utopian ideologies conceptualize their missions as endless, undistracted by short-term success, pursuing rebellion for its own sake. This is the essence of Marcuse's Great Refusal: persistent defiance and ongoing negative action in constant motion so as to remain steps ahead of the deadly pull of one-dimensionality. For the moment the movement basks in its glories, retreads on its victories, or seeks comfort in its habits, its politics become stagnant and routine.

Key to the viability of a human rights community is its creativity and dynamism. Monotony breeds predictability. Again, Nadya and Masha are instructive on this point: "The point of a collective like Pussy Riot is that they aren't going to wait for a formula to be tested; they will continue to act directly and without warning" (Frere-Jones 2014). The hierarchy and bureaucracy endemic to professionalized human rights advocacy impede free thought and inventive solutions. Another crisis, another hashtag, another celebrity, another benefit concert. Rinse and repeat. Breaking out of this mold would have the effect of shaking the audience from the stupor of another campaign ad and another e-mail solicitation. This will require forward-thinking approaches to media and communications strategies that establish unique narratives and motifs. As well, mediated spaces and digital platforms must be constructed so as to bear directly on earthly politics, rather than getting stuck being only for itself. Human rights groups would do well to forge meaningful relationships with communities of artists engaged in social practice and learn from their means and methods. New iterations of human rights advocacy can only emerge by unleashing the creative forces of thoughtful people committed to political change.

Furthermore and finally, cultivating a base of supporters through mass appeals manufactures an anonymous whole of amalgamated, congealed bodies as opposed to a collectivity of self-realized individuals. Because, after all, mass appeals are all about volume. In the pursuit of numbers, NGOs cater to the lowest common denominator, oversimplify complex events, accept members of all partisan persuasions, and utilize products of mass consumption. Eighty years ago, Walter Benjamin warned us of the creeping threat inherent in mass culture: "Quantity has been transmuted into quality. The greatly increased mass of participants has produced a change in the mode of participation" (Benjamin 1968, 239). Human rights should not cast itself as the palatable alternative to ideological politics. Human rights cannot be everything to everyone. There must be some basis for identifying the perspectives that support human rights protection and those that compromise it. Holding firmly, as if through ideological commitment, to the principles upon which human rights is built can position human rights to assume the mantle of the truly "transcendent project" (Marcuse 1964, 220) that it has the potential to be.

Notes

1. "No pasaràn!" translates to "they shall not pass" and is itself an appropriation of the words of Dolores Ibàrruri, a Spanish Marxist leader speaking at an anti-fascist rally opposing the rise of General Francisco Franco at the outset of the Civil War in 1936 (Dellinger 2013).
2. The Situationists were given new life in the late 1990s, as opponents of the globalization of neoliberal capitalism seized on and repurposed corporate logos and slogans in a practice termed "culture jamming" (Lasn 1999).

References

Amnesty International USA. 2014. "Bringing Human Rights Home." Feb 5 Concert, February 5. http://www.amnestyusa.org/Feb5Concert.

Ash, Lucy. 2011. "How Banksy Bailed out Voina." *BBC*, March 5, sec. Europe. http://www.bbc.co.uk/news/world-europe-12645902.

Benjamin, Walter. 1968. "The Work of Art in the Age of Mechanical Reproduction." In *Illuminations: Essays and Reflections*, edited by Hannah Arendt. New York: Harcourt Brace Jovanovich.

Crabapple, Molly. 2014. "A Brief Encounter With Post-Pussy Riot Nadya and Masha." ANIMAL, February 11. http://animalnewyork.com/2014/brief-encounter-post-pussy-riot-nadya-masha.

Dellinger, Mary Ann. 2013. "The Mythopoeia of Dolores Ibarrui, Pasionaria." In *Memory and Cultural History of the Spanish Civil War: Realms of Oblivion*, edited by Kelly DeVries, John France, Michael S. Neiberg, and Frederick Schneid. Leiden: BRILL.

Elder, Miriam. 2014. "What Does Pussy Riot Mean Now?" BuzzFeed, February 7. http://www.buzzfeed.com/miriamelder/what-does-pussy-riot-mean-now.

Erickson, Jon. 1992. "The Spectacle of the Anti-spectacle: Happenings and the Situationist International." *Discourse* 14 (2): 36–58.

Flanary, Patrick. 2013. "Peter Gabriel, Billy Bragg Join the Voice Project's Album for Peace in Africa." Rolling Stone, January 10. http://www.rollingstone.com/music/news/peter-gabriel-billy-bragg-join-the-voice-projects-album-for-peace-in-africa-20130110.

Frere-Jones, Sasha. 2014. "Ready to Die." *The New Yorker*, February 6. http://www.newyorker.com/culture/sasha-frere-jones/ready-to-die.

Galperina, Marina. 2010. "Voina Overturn a Cop Car." ANIMAL, September 20. http://animalnewyork.com/2010/voina-overturn-a-cop-car.

Garadja, Anonymous Members of Pussy Riot, Fara, Shaiba, Cat, Seraphima, and Schumacher. 2014. "We Wish Nadia and Masha Well, But They're No Longer Part of Pussy Riot." *The Guardian*, February 6. http://www.theguardian.com/commentisfree/2014/feb/06/nadia-masha-pussy-riot-collective-no-longer.

Gramsci, Antonio. 1971. *Selections from the Prison Notebooks of Antonio Gramsci*, edited by Geoffrey Nowell-Smith. New York: International Publishers.

Hopgood, Stephen. 2006. *Keepers of the Flame: Understanding Amnesty International*. Ithaca, NY: Cornell University Press.

Knabb, Ken (ed.). 2006. *Situationist International Anthology*. Translated by Ken Knabb. Berkeley, CA: Bureau of Public Secrets.

Lasn, Kalle. 1999. *Culture Jam: The Uncooling of America*, 1st ed. New York: William Morrow and Company.

Marcuse, Herbert. 1964. *One-Dimensional Man*. Boston: Beacon Press.

Ross, Alex. 2014. "Pop Culture and Power." *The New Yorker*, September 8. http://www.newyorker.com/magazine/2014/09/15/naysayers.

Shepherd, Julianne Escobedo. 2014. "Kim Gordon, James Murphy and Jake Gyllenhaal Party for Pussy Riot." Rolling Stone, February 7. http://www.rollingstone.com/culture/news/kim-gordon-james-murphy-and-jake-gyllenhaal-party-for-pussy-riot-20140207.

VOICE Project. 2014. "The Pussy Riot International Support Fund—January 1, 2014 Report." *Voice Project* (blog), January 1. http://voiceproject.org/post_news/the-pussy-riot-international-support-fund-january-1-2014-report.

———. n.d. "Our Story." *Voice Project* (blog). http://voiceproject.org/our-story.

Žižek, Slavoj, and Nadezhda Tolokonnikova. 2013. "Nadezhda Tolokonnikova of Pussy Riot's Prison Letters to Slavoj Žižek." *The Guardian*, November 15. http://www.theguardian.com/music/2013/nov/15/pussy-riot-nadezhda-tolokonnikova-slavoj-zizek.

Index

J. R. Pruce, *The Mass Appeal of Human Rights*, Human Rights Interventions, https://doi.org/10.1007/978-3-319-92075-7

The manufacturer's authorised representative in the EU is Springer Nature Customer Service Centre GmbH, Europaplatz 3, 69115 Heidelberg, Germany. If you have any concerns regarding our products, please contact ProductSafety@springernature.com

Printed and bound by CPI Group (UK) Ltd, Croydon, CR0 4YY
30/09/2026
02225660-0001